John D. Harris
5/02

CORVETTE
1953-1962

Mike Mueller

Motorbooks International
Publishers & Wholesalers

First published in 1996 by Motorbooks International Publishers & Wholesalers, 729 Prospect Avenue, PO Box 1, Osceola WI 54020 USA

Motorbooks International is a certified trademark, registered with the United States Patent Office

The information in this book is true and complete to the best of our knowledge. All recommendations are made without any guarantee on the part of the author or Publisher, who also disclaim any liability incurred in connection with the use of this data or specific details

We recognize that some words, model names and designations, for example, mentioned herein are the property of the trademark holder. We use them for identification purposes only. This is not an official publication

Motorbooks International books are also available at discounts in bulk quantity for industrial or sales-promotional use. For details write to Special Sales Manager at the Publisher's address

Library of Congress Cataloging-in-Publication Data Available

ISBN 0-7603-0041-0

On the front cover: Chevrolet stripped off the bright trunk bands in 1959, but little else was changed in 1959 from a tail point of view. This 1959 Corvette belongs to Bruce and Karen Slattery of Cincinnati, Ohio.

On the frontispiece: The familiar Chevrolet crossed flag emblem adorned the steering wheel of the 1961 Corvette "Big Tank" fuelie. This one is owned by Elmer and Sharon Lash of Champaign, Illinois.

On the title page: This 1958 Corvette fuelie belongs to Dick Hubbard of Monticello, Indiana.

On the back cover: This 1957 Corvette 250hp fuelie belongs to Brent and Janet Ferguson of Orlando, Florida (top). Chevrolet's first production Corvette rolled off the very short makeshift assembly line in Flint, Michigan, on June 30, 1953. Early models used standard Bel Air passenger car wheelcovers because the planned "knock-off" style covers weren't ready in time (bottom).

Printed in Hong Kong

Contents

Acknowledgments

We could still see all the stars even though the Kentucky skies that Thursday night were grey and rainy. Country singer George Jones serenaded us before dinner. And the *Beach Boys* were waiting in the wings to welcome the estimated 100,000 visitors scheduled to start arriving full-force in and around Bowling Green the next day. As for that evening, all the great names were seated around us. Chevrolet general manager Jim Perkins. Chief Corvette engineers Zora Arkus-Duntov, Dave McLellan and Dave Hill. Designer Larry Shinoda. Et cetera, et cetera. For fiberglass fanatics, this was the VIP dinner to end all VIP dinners. After all, you only get one chance to celebrate the grand opening of anything. And "anything" in this case was the National Corvette Museum, the long-awaited Valhalla for Corvette lovers that officially opened on Friday, September 2, 1994.

The feeding frenzy began once the ceremonial ribbon was cut and the faithful started flooding in. By Monday the turnstiles had clicked over 118,047 times. It wasn't exactly a madhouse, but it was close. Luckily I was one of the fortunate folks invited to see the place for myself in less hectic fashion with all those VIPs the night before the grand opening. And it was there that I ran into a good friend, Ray Quinlan, who was beaming like a new father who'd just had triplets.

Ray got invited to that Thursday night VIP reception, too, but for a much different reason than me. I'm not very important at all. I'm a journalist. Ray, on the other hand, simply couldn't be overlooked when it came time to assemble all the people—big, little or otherwise—who helped make that night possible. He was among those who first started the NCM ball rolling long before ground was even broken on the site directly across from the Corvette assembly plant in Bowling Green. Ray was the first to donate a car—appropriately enough, a 1953 Corvette—to the museum collection. He obviously had confidence in the dream when others weren't so sure. In return, he now carries NCM founding membership card number 1, a lifetime honor.

I, too, owe a major debt of gratitude to Ray Quinlan, who was also among those who gave me a break when I was first trying to make it as an automotive writer/photographer. I first got to know Ray after graduating from the University of Illinois in 1983 when I joined his car club in Champaign, Illinois. His supercharged Studebaker Avanti was one of the first cars I photographed for a magazine feature in 1984. Ever since, Ray has been there each time I've looked for help or support, and he has always treated me like family, even going so far as to let me drive his A.C. Cobra two summers ago. I'm sitting at my Macintosh in sunny Florida right now hammering out this book instead of digging ditches somewhere in the frozen north due to people like Ray Quinlan. Thanks, however, is simply not a big enough word. I'll say it anyway, Ray, but not until I see you the next time I'm hunting down some rare car to photograph in the Midwest.

As for all the other very important people who helped make this book possible, where to start? Perhaps at the beginning, say, with my parents, Jim and Nancy Mueller, who also just happen to be my biggest fans—I think. The old Mueller homestead in Illinois outside Champaign has also come in handy many times during the various 5,000-mile photo junkets required to piece this and other epics of mine together. And those trips would've been far more work and much less fun if my various "assistants" hadn't come along now and again. First and foremost is my brother Dave Mueller, who now knows this work probably better than I. But I can't forget my other brothers, Jim Jr. and Ken, as well as my brother-in-law, Illinois State Police Trooper Frank Young, and his boy, Jason. All your overtime was greatly appreciated. The checks are in the mail, honest.

As usual, my former cohorts at the Dobbs Publishing Group here in Lakeland, Florida, were ready, willing and able to let me use and abuse them for my own personal gain. Thanks go to DPG's Donald Farr, who gave me my first full-time job in this field in 1987; *Corvette Fever* editor Greg Pernula, who again let me ransack his files; and former *CF* chief Paul Zazarine, who didn't really do anything for me this time, but I still owe him from many times before.

Rob Reaser, another DPG editor and the hardest working photo technician outside Hollywood, also once again came through when I needed mucho B&W processing and printing work done absolutely, positively overnight. Right up there with Rob is Lakeland's Ollie Young, who opened his darkroom for me on short notice in Reaser's absence.

Noted Corvette expert Noland Adams again saved the day for me on this project, just as he did concerning my 1963-67 Sting Ray book two years ago. Noland is a man of his word, which is probably more than can be said about me.

Historical photographic support came from automotive writer/historians Bob Ackerson and Mike Lamm, veteran West Coast racing photographer Bob Tronolone, and Jonathan Mauk at the Daytona International Speedway archives.

Support of another kind came from various Corvette crazies and collectors around the country who either helped me during photo shoots or pointed me in the right direction when I was looking for a specific car to photograph. Among these friends in Florida are Bill Locke, *Road & Track* photographer Bill Warner, Ed Kuziel, and Brent Ferguson, of the the Classic Corvettes of Orlando Club.

Elsewhere, this list also includes Elmer Lash in Champaign, Illinois; Robin Winnan at Harmony Corvette in Marengo, Illinois; Dick Hubbard, of the Hubbard GM Center in Monticello, Indiana; Ellen Kliene at the Indianapolis Motor Speedway Hall of Fame Museum, Indianapolis, Indiana; musclecar collector Milton Robson and his ace righthand man, Wayne Allen, in Gainesville, Georgia; Chip Miller and all the great folks at Carlisle Productions in Carlisle, Pennsylvania, home to the annual "Corvette at Carlisle" extravaganza; Chip's main man, Paul Cherchuck, also of Carlisle; Tom Biltcliff and Guy Landis, both of Kutztown, Pennsylvania; Terry Michaelis and his guys at Pro Team Corvette Sales in Napoleon, Ohio; and Dan Gale, Danny Gillock, Tim Reilly, and Patrick Hayes at the National Corvette Museum in Bowling Green.

Last, but certainly not least, I must mention another great friend, Bill Tower, in nearby Plant City, Florida. Not only has Bill repeatedly bent over backwards to allow me to photograph his fantastic fiberglass collection (you'll see inside), he has also been a great companion on more than one automotive adventure over the last few years. A former GM engineer and NASCAR race engine builder, he has always been

more than willing to help open doors for me as well. Bill, I know a free lunch for as long as you live isn't quite enough in exchange, but you know me. Say hi to Betty for me, too.

I'm reasonably sure I've left out a name or two in here somewhere. Perhaps I can make it up in my next book, that is if my Motorbooks editors will ever forgive me for this one. Finally, let me not forget all the car owners who gave their time and energy so I could capture their great cars on film for these pages. In general order of appearance, they are:

1953 Muntz Jet, Fred and Lyn Hunter, Ft. Lauderdale, Florida; 1953 Nash-Healey, Paul Sable, Fleetwood, Pennsylvania; 1954 Kaiser-Darrin, Edwin Hobart, Naples, Florida; 1953 Corvette, Chip Miller, Carlisle, Pennsylvania; 1954 Corvette, Bill Warner,

A very proud Ray Quinlan with his 1953 Corvette at the National Corvette Museum in Bowling Green, Kentucky, on the night before the NCM's long-awaited grand opening, September 2, 1994. Ray donated his car to the NCM group long before there was a NCM, becoming one of the first Corvette fanatics to help transform the Bowling Green museum from dream into reality.

Jacksonville, Florida; 1955 Corvette, Elmer and Dean Puckett, Elgin, Illinois; 1956 Corvette, Frank Diefenderfer III, Orlando, Florida; 1956 Corvette SR-2 (Bill Mitchell's) and "Betty Skelton beach racer," Bill and Betty Tower, Plant City, Florida; 1956 Corvette SR-2 (Jerry Earl's), Rich Mason, Carson City, Nevada; 1956 Corvette SR-2 "low-fin" (Harlow Curtice's), Richard and Carolyn Fortier, Swartz Creek, Michigan; 1957 Corvette "Airbox" fuelie, Milton Robson, Gainesville, Georgia; 1957 Corvette 270hp, Bob and Diane Colfer, Macungie, Pennsylvania; 1957 Corvette 250hp fuelie, Brent and Janet Ferguson, Orlando, Florida; 1957 Corvette SS, Indianapolis Motor Speedway Hall of Fame Museum, Indianapolis, Indiana; 1958 Corvette 230hp, Ron Cenowa, Shelby Township, Michigan; 1958 Corvette 245hp, Gary Gudla, Norridge, Illinois; 1958 Corvette fuelie, Dick Hubbard, Monticello, Indiana; 1958 Corvette "retractable hardtop," Terry Michealis, Pro Team Corvette Sales, Napoleon, Ohio; 1959 Corvette, Bruce and Karen Slattery, Cincinnati, Ohio; 1960 Corvette 270hp, Kevin and Sally Waspi, Urbana, Illinois; 1960 Corvette 230hp, Bob and Shirley Stallings, Orlando, Florida; 1961 Corvette 230hp, Steve Weimer, Weston, Florida; 1961 Corvette "Big Tank" fuelie, Elmer and Sharon Lash, Champaign, Illinois; 1962 Corvette 250hp, Bob and Shirley Stallings, Orlando, Florida; 1962 Corvette 340hp, Doug and Lee Mann, Bourbannais, Illinois; 1962 Corvette SCCA racer, Tim and Carol Partridge, South Barrington, Illinois.

Thanks to all.

Chapter 1

Introduction
Speaking Of Sports

Calling Chevrolet's Corvette "America's only sports car" was for years a relatively quick way to start an argument, especially with those indefatigable souls who forever subscribe to the belief that a sports car is only a sports car if it both taxes and excites the senses. Wind-in-your hair thrills must also bring along rain-down-your-neck compromises. Up-close-and-personal two-seat grand touring should also mean knocking knees and elbows. Roll-up glass windows? Hell no; it has to be side curtains or nothing at all. And if you're not forced to carry a tool kit along on every ride, you're simply not driving a true sports car.

Of course, that rudimentary ideal, once prominent in the heyday of the fabled, finicky British sports car, has long since lost favor as technological advances and basic changes in taste have redefined the way the world looks at sporty automobiles—and automobiles in general, for that matter. Today, the top world sports cars offer the best of everything; few, if any, compromises here. That the certainly classy, relatively comfortable, reasonably-luxurious Corvette is a true sports car has been a foregone conclusion for quite a few years now; not so early on.

As for the "America's only" aspect, that too has required some liberal interpretation over the years. Many sports-minded devotees—from those

Before the sensational Sting Ray, there were the so-called "solid-axle" Corvettes, the first-generation models built between 1953 and 1962. This 1962 edition shows off the same quad-headlight nose that graced the solid-axle cars for the last five years of that production run.

American sports cars were, to say the least, rare in postwar era before the Corvette came along. Although not exactly a sports car by the book—it was too large and had an equally large backseat—the Muntz Jet was a sporty machine born of a sports car. Before Earl "Madman" Muntz bought the rights to produce this car in 1949 it was a product of the Kurtis-Kraft company. Veteran racer Frank Kurtis originally created the vehicle in 1949. When first built by Kurtis, the car rolled on a shorter wheelbase and had only two seats

lucky enough to have experienced the rarely seen Nash-Healey Euro-Yankee hybrid in the early 1950s, to ponycar promoters hot on AMC's two-seat AMX in 1968, to today's victims of the Dodge Viper's venom—just might have a bone to pick with Chevy's hypemasters for making that bold claim. Yet when you consider no automaker in this country has ever done it any better, or for anywhere near as long as Chevrolet has now for more than four decades, it becomes easier to overlook the Bow-Tie boys' over-enthusiasm. Sure, a better description might be "America's only long successful sports car"—no, Viper fans, Dodge hasn't proven spit yet. But it's only right to continue bestowing upon the Corvette an honor it has for some time deserved simply for being out there and proving it all night. "America's only sports car" isn't a dictionary definition, it's a statement.

Earning that honor took more than a few years of hard work, both on the street and at the track. After struggling for its very life during its first three years, Chevrolet's fiberglass two-seater then took flight in a flurry in 1956, and continued gaining altitude each successive year as performance improved and a competition reputation grew—at least from a purely American perspective. Sport-minded chaps overseas, however, continued pooh-poohing the car, as did some Yankees here at home who still believed that only Brits, Germans and Italians could build real sports cars.

Those biases began to fall in a big way in 1963 with the arrival of the all-new Sting Ray, a stunning redesign that did its first-generation forerunners, built from 1953 to 1962, more than one better with its sleek, timeless lines and state-of-the-art (in American terms) independent rear suspension. Even long-time Corvette chief engineer Zora Arkus-Duntov was finally fully impressed. "For the first time," he commented to the press, "I now have a Corvette I can be proud to drive in Europe."

Racer Frank Kurtis with his Kurtis-Kraft sports car, built in California from late 1949 through 1950. Its body was mostly aluminum and power, in most cases, came from a "hopped-up" Ford flathead V-8. Only 36 were built before Earl Muntz bought Kurtis' factory and moved it to Evanston, Illinois.

A slap at the first-generation Corvette? Although it certainly did sound like one, what Duntov meant was that his baby had finally reached a goal he had been chasing seriously since 1957; the Corvette had become a world-class sports car, at least in the opinion of many more curbside critics than ever before. That achievement, however, did not diminish gains made previously. After all, progress can only be progress if the first step is taken.

Sure, the first-generation Corvettes had their glitches. Total weight was a bit much in comparison to foreign rivals. Brakes were never quite up to snuff. And the yeoman-like chassis was always limited considerably—even with top racing options—by that meat-and-potatoes live axle in back. Nonetheless, the so-called "solid-axle" Corvettes did represent more driving excitement than most Americans would ever experience—on U.S. roads and racetracks, they were all but unbeatable.

Most importantly, they were true pioneers on the Detroit scene. They represented a totally new kind of performance, a sensual brand of speed that bridged the gap between the existing foreign sports car ideal and the expectations, as well as demands,

The Muntz Jet featured its radio mounted in a center console between two "bucket" seats, representing the first modern console/bucket arrangement in an American car. Also notice the seatbelts and padded dash, two more innovative features.

of this country's typical drivers. As it was, most Americans couldn't have cared less about whether or not the early Corvette qualified by accepted sporting standards since so few customers in those days had even seen an honest-to-goodness sports car, let alone driven one.

Sports cars in America were still a rare breed in the days just prior to the Corvette's birth in January 1953. U.S. registrations of sporty two-seaters amounted to only 11,199 in 1952, a nearly unnoticeable figure that represented ever so slightly more than one-quarter of one percent of the total 4.16 million automobiles registered on these shores that year. Of that relatively meager sum, 7,449 were MG TDs, the latest lovely little roadster from Morris Garages, the British builder that had turned more than one Yankee serviceman's head with its carefree two-seaters in England during World War II. Second behind the TD at 3,349 registrations was Jaguar's classic XK120, a more expensive, much more powerful sporting machine compared to its fellow countryman from MG.

At a glance, these statistics didn't exactly support the notion that sports cars were turning many heads here in the States in those days. But, among others, Zora Duntov didn't believe that numbers told the whole story, which he tried to explain in a 1953 address before the Society of Automotive Engineers. "Considering the statistics," he said, "the American public does not want a sports car at all. But do the statistics give a true picture? As far as the American market is concerned, it is still an unknown quantity, since an American sports car catering to American tastes, roads, ways of living and national character has not yet been on the market."

Duntov wasn't the first in this country to speak out in defense of the sports car. Legendary automotive journalist Ken Purdy had, four years before, predicted that a sporty flair would soon be finding its way into Detroit's hum-drum, everyday automobiles. Again. In a 1949 *True* magazine feature entitled "The Two-Seater Comes Back," he told of how everything that goes around probably comes around:

"Before the Kaiser War, when Americans were serious about their motoring, the fast, high-performance two-seater automobile was as common as the 5-cent schooner of beer, and a lot more fun. But time passed, and inevitably the U.S. automobile began to change from an instrument of sport, like a pair of skis, into a device for economical mass transportation, and the two-seater was lost

in the shuffle. Comes now a cloud on the horizon bigger than a man's hand which may portend a revival on this side of the water of the sports car—an automobile built for the sole purpose of going like a bat out of hell and never mind whether the girl friend likes it or not."

That Purdy found himself reaching back 35 years into the glory days of big, burly stripped-down machines like the Mercer Raceabout and Stutz Bearcat for a point of reference did not mean Americans were not treated to a little taste of speed in the years between the two World Wars. While sporty two-seat travel was indeed almost non-existent during those years, performance machines were available, although primarily only to the very rich. The Great Depression then changed all that, doing in, among others, the classic Auburn-Cord-Duesenberg triumvirate, which had been among the 1930s leaders in both power and price. And once World War II helped wipe the slate clean even further, the U.S. market was left open for whatever new form of travel buyers would accept. Sports cars perhaps?

Argosy's Ralph Stein thought so. "There is no good reason why America should not be able to produce a good sports car," he wrote in 1950. "We have engineers and designers with enough on the ball to create a crackerjack car, but, from observations, it looks very much as if they don't know what it takes. With a fast-growing band of sports-car fans, however, the demand will gradually make itself felt."

But that demand was at first considerably slow in coming as the 1950s dawned, for various reasons. Yes, some military men had brought back the sports car bug from Europe in 1945 and 1946. Most, however, remained immune as resuming (or starting) their family life was the main priority—a two-seater was definitely out of the question once kids came into the picture. On top of that, typical American car buyers with typical American car-buying budgets had yet to discover that there was nothing wrong with expecting a little pizzazz along with their practical transportation. And since they weren't exactly asking for such a combination, Detroit wasn't in any particular hurry to offer it.

Yet there were small pockets of sporty car interest present during the early postwar years. One of these was nurtured by U.S. Air Force General Curtis LeMay, who hoped to help boost military morale by arranging sports car races at various Strategic Air Command bases. A good friend of General Motors Styling head Harley Earl, it was LeMay who reportedly put a bug in Earl's ear concerning the prospects of GM building a true sports car. Also helping further the cause was the Sports Car Club of America (SCCA), which in its first years immediately following the end of World War II essentially only showcased foreign cars since domestic counterparts were essentially nowhere to be found.

Probably the first real American sports car of the postwar era was the Nash-Healey. Representing a meeting of the minds of Nash-Kelvinator's George Mason and British racer Donald Healey, the Nash-Healey featured a warmed-over Nash six-cylinder engine, a Healey-prepared chassis and Italian coachwork from Pinin Farina. Only 506 Nash-Healey sportsters, roadsters and coupes, were built from 1951 to 1954. Some leftover coupes were sold as 1955 models.

Commonly taking the credit for leading the foreign sports car wave (actually, it was more like a ripple) onto these shores was MG; again an arguable claim, but a presumption that does help explain the aforementioned relative popularity of the TD by 1952. Introduced to the U.S. market in 1950, the TD had picked up where the cute, little MG TC, born in 1945, had left off. Americans loved them, even with their cramped quarters, crude soft-tops and weak-kneed four-cylinder power. Of the 29,664 TDs built between late 1949 and 1953, 23,488 were imported to this country.

Jaguar's first XK120 reached the East Coast in August 1949. Priced at about $3,500, nearly twice as much as the MG TD, the long, low XK120 didn't draw nearly as much as attention, at least not at first. But what few early looks it garnered it did for good reason. With a 160- or 180-hp dual-overhead-cam six-cylinder be-tween those flowing fenders, a top end of 120mph was a distinct possibility—thus the car's name.

Yet another British manufacturer, Triumph, jumped into the game in 1953 with its familiar TR-2, a 90-mph sportster priced at around $2,300, a little more than the MG, a lot less than the Jag. An additional $600 or so that year bought a fourth two-seater from England, Austin Healey's new 100/4, a thoroughly modern-looking brute of a sports car that could really satisfy an American driver's need for speed.

German contributions to the sports car invasion in the early 1950s included Porsche's 356 and the Mercedes-Benz SL models. Even higher up on the rich boy's playtoy scale were the truly exotic, hand-built Italian specials from Maserati and Ferrari.

U.S. responses to the European offensive? While Duntov wasn't entirely correct in 1953 when he said an American sports car "has not yet been on the market," early postwar attempts in this country to build and market a successful sporty machine were certainly easy to overlook. Right out of the blocks, we can forget all about the host of small-time, privately built sportsters that came and went in the late 1940s and early 1950s like spent lottery tickets in a windswept convenience store parking lot.

Earliest of note from a "major" manufacturer was the Crosley Hot Shot, yet another tiny offering from National League baseball team (Cincinnati Reds) owner and refrigerator magnate Powel Crosley. Wearing no doors and an equally small price tag of about $860, the two-seat Hot Shot debuted in 1949, powered by a 26.5hp four-cylinder engine. Optional doors were added in 1950, creating the Super Sport. Neither versions were ever really given serious consideration, nor was the Crosley firm itself. It was history by the end of 1952.

Debuting as well in 1949 was an intriguing two-seat convertible conceived by veteran race car builder Frank Kurtis. His California-based company, Kurtis-Kraft, attempted to market his slab-sided creation, which was powered by a Ford flathead V-8 commonly spruced up with an aftermarket hot rod piece or two. On top was a low, clean body made of mostly aluminum. Kurtis' cars impressed many with their speed potential, including Ken Purdy, whose aforementioned *True* article featured one, along with a Crosley Hot Shot and a Jaguar XK120. Although Purdy was told that Kurtis-Kraft production would reach about 300 models a year, only 36 cars were built before Kurtis sold everything to renowned used car dealer Earl "Madman" Muntz. After briefly continuing production of his own modified version of the car in California, Muntz then moved production to Evanston, Illinois.

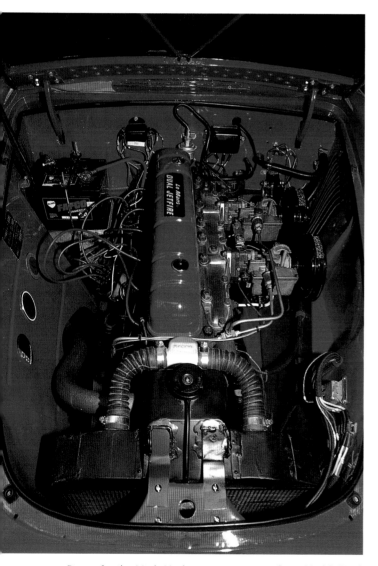

Power for the Nash-Healey sports car came from Nash's Dual Jetfire Le Mans six-cylinder, a 252ci engine that produced 135hp. The twin-carb Dual Jetfire Le Mans six was also an option for the Nash Ambassador in 1953 and 1954.

Originally conceived by legendary stylist Howard "Dutch" Darrin, the Kaiser-Darrin was built by independent automaker Henry J. Kaiser at the urging of his wife in 1954. Its fiberglass body wasn't its only innovative feature. The Darrin's soft top could fold halfway down in landau fashion and its doors disappeared forward into the front fenders.

In the hands of the Madman, the convertible's wheelbase was stretched by about a foot, aluminum was traded for steel, a custom Carson top replaced Kurtis' folding unit, a backseat was added, and horsepower was upped considerably—first by a 331ci Cadillac V-8, then eventually by Lincoln's excellent 317ci overhead-valve V-8 after it debuted in 1952. Completing the package was a new name—Muntz Jet. Even while falling a reported $1,000 behind on each car sold, Madman Muntz still managed to build roughly 500 of his speedy Jets before finally cutting his losses. The very last Muntz Jet was built in 1954.

While the 160hp Muntz Jet was definitely a hot performance car, was it a sports car? No, not considering its size, weight, corresponding big-

car handling and the plain fact that it had more than two seats. It does, however, deserve credit for making a major contribution to sporty car design: the Muntz Jet apparently was the first American postwar car to show off a modern console/bucket seat combination. A padded dash and standard seat belts represented two other ground-breaking features.

If any one automobile did deserve credit as this country's first postwar sports car it was the Nash-Healey, a hybrid that at least was part American. A brilliant combination of British chassis, Yankee drivetrain and Italian bodywork, the Nash-Healey represented the meeting of minds between Nash-Kelvinator's George Mason and famed British sports car builder Donald Healey.

Certainly small, even by accepted sports car standards of the day, Powel Crosley's Hot Shot debuted in 1949 as a carefree, inexpensive sportabout. Doors were later added, creating the Super Sport. Crosley built these four-cylinder-powered roller skates up through 1952, the last year for his automaking venture. *courtesy Robert Ackerson*

If Crosley's Hot Shot or Super Sport didn't trick a budget-conscious buyer's trigger there was always the Skorpion fiberglass body kit, which first appeared in 1950. Ranging from about $450 to $600, the Skorpion kit could drop right onto a Crosley chassis.

The idea behind the Nash-Healey was launched in December 1949 aboard the *Queen Elizabeth*, then heading west across the Atlantic from England to America. Both Mason and Healey were aboard, the latter bound for the U.S. in search of a suitable American engine to power an export model he wanted to build. A chance meeting ensued, inspiring Mason to make a proposal: why not use Nash's overhead-valve six-cylinder as the base for this new sports car? Healey would get his horses—125 to be exact—while Mason would reap the rewards of a high-performance image, something Nash automobiles weren't exactly dripping with in the early 1950s. Healey agreed and the two company names then became joined at the hyphen.

A competition prototype using Nash's 234ci six and a 102-inch wheelbase Healey chassis was built in 1950 and raced at Le Mans that year, finishing fourth overall. More than 100 production versions with British-built bodies were then rolled out in 1951. Not fond of the body used that year, Mason then contracted Pinin Farina—the Italian coachworks that had created Nash's new regular-production body for 1952—to reshape the Nash-Healey sportster into a more distinctive machine. Although the results were certainly worthy of the Pinin Farina badge, the Nash-Healey convertible never really caught on with American buyers. Nor did the Nash-Healey coupe, which joined the lineup in 1953 and carried on alone into 1954. Production finally ended in August that year, with only 506 Nash-Healeys built over the four-year run. A handful of the 90 coupes built for 1954 ended up as "leftover" 1955 models.

About the time the Nash-Healey was rolling off into the sunset, another American sports car was just coming into being. And again the manufacturer was an independent, not one of Detroit's "Big Three."

Called "The Sports Car the World Has Been Awaiting," the Kaiser-Darrin was a distinct departure from the more practical product line Henry J. Kaiser had been offering since 1946. Actually, Henry J. reportedly wanted nothing to do with this idea when he first saw it in the California studio of Howard "Dutch" Darrin, he of prewar Packard fame. Darrin had been with Kaiser-Frazer off and on during the independent automakers early years, and was then "off" in 1952 when he borrowed a chassis from a Henry J—Kaiser's little compact car named after the boss—and used it as a base for the sports car Mr. Kaiser didn't like. Initially. Reportedly, Mrs. Kaiser, on the other hand, was thoroughly impressed. And it was she who, legend has it, whispered in hubbie's ear that he should build this car.

That he did, beginning in December 1953. Rolling on a 100-inch wheelbase, the long, low, rakish Kaiser-Darrin featured a three-position folding landau top, wire wheelcovers and curious doors that, instead of swinging open, disappeared

Chapter 2

1953-55
Born In A Rush

That America's only sports car has been running strong now through four generations for more than four decades stands as an impressive achievement on its own, given the constant tugs and shoves of an ever-changing market. Almost cut loose in its early years when demand failed to materialize as planned, Chevrolet's Corvette did manage to find its niche, and has with ease survived at least one major malaise, that coming in the second half of the 1970s. An all-new fifth-generation Corvette is being readied for release even as you gaze at the pictures on these pages, all this happening while rumors still persist concerning a final end of the road for Chevy's fiberglass two-seater. Or at least a trip down an off ramp as plans to merge the F-body Camaro and upscale Corvette have been discussed.

Long forgotten, yet far more amazing than the car's longevity record, was the short time Chevrolet originally required to create the Corvette some 40 years ago. In most cases, simply updating an existing model line in Detroit requires maybe three years or so. The typical time needed to kick off an entirely new breed is anyone's guess, but obviously you can start at "years," plural.

From initial sketches to the first Corvette off the production line in June 1953 incredibly amounted to less than 18 months—and this for an untried ideal (for a major postwar manufac-

All 300 1953 Corvettes were painted Polo White with red interiors. That "toothy" grille would remain a trademark up through 1960. Wearing 13 teeth from 1953 to 1955, it would loose four of those beginning in 1958.

One way to identify a 1953 Corvette is by its black canvas top; the color was changed to beige in 1954. Also notice the short, stubby exhaust tips. These were lengthened on 1954 models, undoubtedly in an attempt cure an exhaust staining problem on the rear bodywork.

turer) that, at a glance, didn't stand much of a chance of gaining a foothold in the American consciousness of the time. This was a sports car, after all, a machine that served no purpose whatsoever other than making merry. Even more incredulous was the fact that this fun-mobile was a Chevrolet, long a low-priced sales leader. "Yeoman" was a fair description for most Chevrolet models in the early 1950s, although "dull" would've certainly worked in a pinch.

Yet there it was, Chevrolet's first Corvette, that somewhat unsure progenitor of more than 1 million more fiberglass two-seaters to follow over the succeeding 40-something years. If you were lucky enough to have bought one in 1953, you could've had a Corvette in any color you liked— as long as you liked Polo White. Same went for the Sportsman Red interior. Equipment choices

were limited as well; the one-and-only power source was the "Blue Flame" six-cylinder backed by a Powerglide automatic transmission. A humble beginning, yes, but it was a beginning.

Responsibility for this hastily prepared product launch was typically shared by so many, from Chevrolet general manager Thomas Keating on down; the division's chief engineer Ed Cole, r&d's Maurice Olley, body engineer Ellis "Jim" Premo, and stylist Robert McLean to name just a few. As much as devoted fiberglass followers today like to respectfully refer to Zora Arkus-Duntov as the "father of the Corvette," he didn't arrive at General Motors until May 1953, four months after the car's public debut in prototype form.

But if any one man does deserve credit for single-handedly starting the Corvette ball rolling it has to be Harley Earl, longtime head of General Motors

Styling. A big man at GM, literally and figuratively, it was Earl who used his weight to push his dream for an American sports car into production.

Dream cars were nothing new for the six-foot-four Stanford graduate, who in the 1920s began his career in California designing custom bodies for some of Hollywood's flashiest characters while working for Los Angeles Cadillac dealer Don Lee. There, Earl was discovered by GM president Alfred Sloan, who brought him to Detroit to work for bodybuilder Lawrence Fisher. As a Fisher Body man, one of Earl's first responsibilities was to create a compelling look for the 1927 LaSalle, Cadillac's new, less-expensive running mate. The results were classic, and the LaSalle has since been called Detroit's first truly styled automobile.

Impressed by what a few well-planned good looks could do for his products' image, Sloan then founded GM's Art and Colour Section on June 23, 1927, and made Earl its head. Just like that, Sloan had taken automobile design responsibilities out of the hands of engineers and given them to Earl's 50-man staff, a move that both signaled an end to the era of independent coachworks and helped boost Earl to greatness. Once his greatness reached sufficient prominence, he took it on himself to paint over the Art and Colour sign, changing that "sissy name" to "Styling Section" in 1937. And with that stroke, he and his people then became "stylists."

The list of stylists who rose to greatness on their own after tutoring under Earl is long. Notables include Virgil Exner, he of Chrysler's "Forward Look;" Frank Hershey, responsible for Ford's Thunderbird and Crown Victoria in 1955; Buick's Ned Nickles; Clare MacKichan, credited with Chevy's legendary "Hot One" of 1955; and William Mitchell, who became Harley's "favored son" and eventually replaced Earl at the top of GM Styling in 1958.

Under Earl's directions, GM stylists put Detroit's first tailfins on the Cadillac in 1948, then started adding trendy wraparound windshields to various models five years later. Earl himself was also responsible for Detroit's first "dream car," the stunning Buick Y-Job. Built in 1938, the Y-Job not only featured futuristic hideaway headlights and an exceptionally clean body devoid of running boards, it also dramatically demonstrated Earl's faith in long, low lines. Later in a 1954 interview he touched on the logic behind this style:

"My primary purpose has been to lengthen and lower the American automobile, at times in reality and always at least in appearance. Why? Because my sense of proportion tells me that oblongs are more attractive than squares, just as a ranch house is more attractive than a square, three-story, flat-roofed house. Or a greyhound is more graceful than a bulldog."

The early Corvette dash—which carried over in basically the same fashion up though 1957—may have appeared sporty looking, but was far from sports-car functional. Tach location was especially poor—it's the large round pod at the bottom of the instrument panel directly in the center.

The early Corvette's Blue Flame six breathed in its good air through three bullet-shaped inlets that were filters in name alone. Low hood clearance influenced various engine compartment installations, including, most prominently, the carburetors. Three side-draft Carters fit nicely on a special aluminum intake manifold.

Projects like the Y-Job then helped inspire yet another new practice for GM, this one involving the way the corporation introduced its products—and products-to-be. General Motors' first Motorama auto show was held in January 1949 in New York's Waldorf-Astoria hotel, kicking off a proud tradition that would serve its purpose well throughout the 1950s as a public proving grounds of sorts. Motorama stages quickly became the best places to see the latest automotive ideas from GM, some far-fetched, others ably predicting the future ahead.

Showcars then became a passion of Earl's, as were sports cars and racing. In 1950 and early 1951, he oversaw the production of two more experimental machines, Buick's LeSabre and XP-300, both sporty, albeit large, two-seaters.

A serious idea for a GM-built, regular-production, two-seater first came to Earl late in 1951. In this case, he envisioned more of a true sports car, a vehicle both relatively small in stature and price. While foreign sports cars, like Jaguar's XK120, did serve as inspiration, so too did the newly introduced Willys Jeepster, a perky, practical, open-air machine priced at less than $2,000. But Earl knew the only way to build a comparably priced GM sportster

would be to keep production costs low by, say, using an existing chassis and/or other components right off the shelf. His idea initially went no further than a few private sketches and a bit of model building in hushed surroundings.

Earl's plan finally came into the light after he saw the fiberglass-bodied Alembic I during its showing on the 11th floor of GM's Styling's Milwaukee Avenue offices in the spring of 1952. Now ready for real action, he escalated his approach, bringing in Bob McLean and assigning him the task of establishing the basic parameters for the head stylist's latest dream machine.

McLean's drawings depicted a low, two-place sportster with a wide stance and a short 102-inch wheelbase. Engine location was key. Using Chevrolet's existing six-cylinder inline powerplant as a model, McLean placed it about three inches lower and seven inches closer to the dash than in typical Chevy installations. An externally mounted spare, reminiscent of the Jeepster's, was first considered, then dropped to help keep things clean in back. Earl's direct contributions to the initial layout included the trendy wraparound windshield and clear headlight cov-

Most innocent bystanders never even noticed the arrival of the second-edition Corvette in 1954, basically since it appeared almost identical to its rarely seen 1953 forerunner. Chevrolet officials at the time didn't even bother to differentiate the two officially in writing.

Various changes here and there help differentiate a 1954 Corvette from a 1953, but the easiest at a glance from the outside involves the lengthened exhaust tips used in 1954—compare these tips to the ones appearing on the 1953 model shown on page 24.

ers that fared the recessed headlamps into the rounded fenders.

Momentum quickly gathered from there. A lifesize clay mockup was hastily prepared in April 1952, followed equally as quick by a full-sized plaster model, which was then shown to Ed Cole. Cole was ecstatic and immediately promised his complete support for the project. Cole and Thomas Keating then showed the model to GM president Harlow Curtice with hopes of receiving Curtice's approval for plans to build an experimental version for the upcoming 1953 Motorama at New York's Waldorf-Astoria in January. He approved.

Next came the engineers. On June 2, Maurice Olley's research and development crew were shown the model and asked to create a suitable chassis. According to Olley, "the need was to produce a sports car, using components of known reliability, with adequate performance, a comfortable ride, and stable handling qualities, in something less than seven months before showing, and 12 months before production." No problem. A mere 10 days later, Olley had already sketched the basic chassis layout—code-named "Opel"—a drawing that all but predicted the final product to the letter. Along the way, Chevrolet officially named the car "Corvette," a moniker borrowed from a lightly protected, lightly armed war-

The Corvette's 235ci Blue Flame six was rated at 150 horsepower in 1953 and through early 1954 production, as advertised on the valve cover of this 1954 model. A cam change then boosted output to 155hp for remaining 1954 Corvettes and the few six-cylinder models built for 1955.

ship class built both during World War II and long before in the days of wooden-hulled sailing vessels.

Olley's chassis design featured a very rigid, yet reasonably light X-member frame with fully boxed side rails. Weight was slightly more than 200 pounds. While front suspension featured many stock Chevy pieces, rear suspension was by leaf springs created specially to help locate the rear axle since modern Hotchkiss drive was used in place of the standard Chevrolet's torque tube. A short, 36-inch-long driveshaft delivered engine torque to a modified stock rearend that featured rebound straps to keep excess travel under control. Rear axle ratio was 3.55:1.

Per standard specs, front shock absorbers were mounted inside the coil springs squeezed between the typical A-arms. The front stabilizer bar, however, was larger than stock and mounted differently than in passenger car applications. Brakes were also off-the-shelf Chevy units, with 11-inch drums at all four corners. Steering was by a Saginaw worm-and-sector box featuring a mildly quick 16:1 ratio.

With Chevrolet's first modern V-8 still two years away, Cole's engineers were left with no choice but to rely on Chevy's yeoman-like "Stovebolt" six-cylinder engine, which by 1953 at least featured lightweight aluminum pistons and improved lubrication and more durable main bearings. Displacing 235 cubic inches, this tried-and-true, overhead-valve inline six produced 115 horsepower at 3600rpm in standard passenger car trim—just fine for everyday transportation, but not near enough to put the sports in sports car.

Again, no problem. Various modifications transformed Chevy's thrifty six-cylinder into the Blue Flame six, a Jekyll and Hyde transformation if there ever was one. Top Blue Flame horsepower was 150hp at 4200rpm, while maximum torque output went from the stock six's 204lb-ft at 2000rpm to 223 at 2400 revs. How'd they do it?

For starters, compression was raised from 7.5:1 to 8:1 and a more aggressive solid-lifter cam was stuffed inside with a .405-inch lift on the intake end, .414 on the exhaust. A metal cam gear replaced the stock fiber piece, all the better to let this powerplant rev beyond 5000rpm and survive to rev again. Valvetrain gear was also beefed with dual valve springs and stronger exhaust valves.

Three Carter one-barrel carburetors—mounted in horizontal sidedraft fashion in order to stay clear of the car's low hood—fed fuel/air to those six combustion chambers through a special aluminum intake manifold. Although three round air cleaners were originally used in the prototype application, they were replaced in production by a trio of small "air inlet extensions." Handling exhaust chores was a split manifold dumping into dual pipes and mufflers.

Additional special features included a "high-efficiency" water pump and shielding for the distributor and plug wires. The latter was added to prevent ignition voltage from wrecking havoc with radio reception since fiberglass panels don't suppress this interference the way typical steel bodies do. As for the high-volume water pump, it was relocated low on the front of the Corvette engine to again allow more hood clearance, this time for the four-bladed fan.

Also mounted low for obvious reasons, the Blue Flame six's radiator required a remote header tank, which on the Motorama prototype was located on the driver's side of the valve cover running parallel with the engine. In regular production, this tank was switched to the opposite side. Yet another change from showcar to streetcar involved the carbs; the Motorama prototype's automatic choke was exchanged for a cable-operated manual setup in production.

Behind the Blue Flame six went the un-sports-car-like two-speed Powerglide automatic transmission, a choice that may have made purists cringe but represented the simplest, least costly (from an engineering standpoint) way of putting the driveline together on such short notice. Powerglide modifications for the Corvette application included a revised tail housing (since a driveshaft was used in place of the standard torque tube) and some internal beefing (shift points came at higher rpm) to better handle the additional engine torque. If it was any consolation, at least the Corvette Powerglide was equipped with a floor-mounted shift lever.

On top of all this went a GRP bodyshell hand-laid in plaster moulds pulled from McLean's original clay model. But while fiberglass would, of course, end up the material of choice for regular-production bodies, it wasn't exactly the first choice. As Jim Premo later told the SAE, "the body on the show model was made of reinforced plastic purely as an expedient to get the job built quickly. At the time of the Waldorf Show, we were actually concentrating on a steel body utilizing Kirksite tooling." Kirksite dies were cheaper and could be fabricated quicker than typical steel dies, but, on the downside, had much shorter working lives. All that, however, was rendered moot once Chevrolet people gained confidence in both the new GRP material's merits and the construction techniques behind its successful use.

Once on its stage at the New York Motorama in January 1953, Chevrolet's GRP-bodied Corvette prototype was turning heads with ease, both with its intriguing fresh face and its apparent state-of-the-art makeup. "People seemed to be captivated by the idea of the fiberglass plastic body," explained Premo. "Furthermore, information being given to us by the reinforced plastic industry seemed to indicate the practicability of fabricating plastic body parts for automobiles on a large scale."

Beyond that, the public was simply in awe of the little Polo White sports car with its low, wide stance, "toothy" grille, wire-mesh stone guards over recessed headlights, wraparound windshield, gloriously red two-seat interior, and dual exhaust tips exiting through its rounded tail. Prospective buyers almost immediately began clamoring for Corvettes of their own right away. Reportedly, original Chevrolet plans called for a production run of 10,000 two-seaters in 1954. Customers wouldn't wait, however, convincing officials to kick off a limited run of 300 'glass-bodied 1953 models that June, meaning Premo and his men had less than six months to get their GRP act in gear.

GM then began accepting bids for the production of Corvette bodies. U.S Rubber, working through GM's Fisher Body Division, tried its hand with a bid, as did the Molded Fiber Glass Company, located in Ashtabula, Ohio. Although the Ohio firm won the contract, worth a reported $4 million, it wasn't exactly prepared for the job. The company's founder, Robert Morrison, first had to establish a second plant, the Molded Fiber Glass Body Company, itself founded in April 1953. He then had to scramble to assemble the various equipment needed to produce the requested GRP panels fast enough. For more than a year, the MFG Body Company relied on a subcontractor to help meet its contract as Morrison's own fiberglass body process wasn't fully up and running until July 1954.

All told, the Corvette's various GRP body parts weighed 340 pounds. Once fabricated in Ohio, they were shipped to GM's makeshift assembly line in Flint, Michigan, where they were glued together and

Another mid-year production change for 1954 involved exchanging the three small air inlets atop the Carter carburetors for a more functional air cleaner arrangement featuring two round filter housings.

finished by hand. The completed body weighed in at 411 pounds and was mated to the chassis at eleven mounting points.

The first of 300 regular-production 1953 Corvettes rolled off the short, temporary Flint line on June 30, 1953, looking very much like the Motorama prototype save for various minor exceptions, some already detailed here. On the outside, the showcar had "Corvette" identification on its nose and tail and "Chevrolet" badges accompanied by a small trim piece on each front fender. Production cars did not have the nose and tail i.d., and their bodyside "Chevrolet" badges were joined by a long trim piece that ran from wheel opening to wheel opening. Headlamp bezels and wheelcovers were different on the showcar, which also featured exterior door pushbuttons and small "scoops" atop each fender—both these features were deleted in production.

Deleted as well were the Motorama model's various chrome touch-ups on the engine, the fan shroud under the hood, and the hydraulic assists for both the hood and doors. On the flipside, additions made to production models included windshield end seals and drip mouldings also with seals. Inside, the showcar's chrome door knobs and painted upper dash edge were exchanged for white knobs and a vinyl-trimmed dash.

As mentioned, all 300 Flint-built 1953 Corvettes were painted Polo White with contrasting red interiors. And all were identically equipped, again save for a few less-than-earth-shaking running changes here and there. The most notable—at

Gypsy Red was reportedly the second most popular Corvette color in 1955, a year when only 700 fiberglass two-seaters were built. Although paint choices had been introduced in 1954, the original Polo White finish dominated that year, and it remained the top choice in 1955.

least on the car itself—came at all four wheels. With tooling of the Corvette's "spinner" wheelcover then apparently not complete, the earliest cars off the line wore covers pirated from passenger-line Bel Airs. According to estimates, at least the first 25 Corvettes were so equipped.

The most prominent "running change" involved the Corvette's production site. From the be-

ginning, the Flint assembly line had served only as a stop-gap measure while Chevrolet officials prepared a more suitable production area at GM's St. Louis assembly plant. St. Louis plant manager William Mosher had been informed in March 1953 that his facility would become home to Corvette production. And it was there that the first 1954 Corvette was completed on December 29,

All Corvettes in 1953 and 1954 and most in 1955 featured two-speed Powerglide automatic transmissions—notice the small Powerglide shift lever on this 1955 model. A long-awaited manual transmission, a three-speed, was first offered in 1955, but only about 70 or 80 were installed.

1953. Reportedly, 15 1954 Corvettes were built that month in St. Louis before production really got rolling in January.

Distinguishing between those 300 1953 Corvettes and the following 1954 models wasn't all that easy at first glance, save for the addition of new exterior paint choices and interior trim shades. While nearly 85 percent of the 1954 Corvette population still featured the Polo White paint with red interior, Chevrolet also introduced Pennant Blue and Sportsman Red exterior finishes, along with Shoreline Beige and blue interior trim. Black paint was also apparently introduced, although in somewhat mysterious fashion. Non-documented estimates claim 1954 exterior color breakdown came to about 300 blue cars, roughly 100 red and perhaps less than 10 black. Factory paperwork in 1954 briefly mentioned Metallic Green and Metallic Bronze paint as well, but both are unknown. Chevrolet also changed the rubberized canvas convertible top color in 1954, replacing black with beige. Reportedly some early 1954 Corvettes may have come with the 1953 black top.

Discounting various hard-to-find technical changes, made both as St. Louis production began

Big news in 1955 was the arrival of more Corvette power, courtesy of Chevrolet's all-new overhead-valve 265ci V-8. Output for the bechromed Corvette 265 was 195hp.

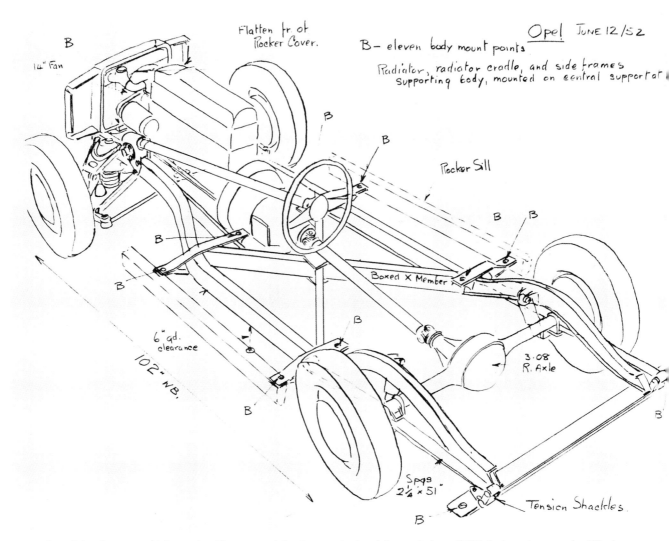

Research and development chief Maurice Olley penned the Corvette's chassis layout in June 1952. Early code name for Olley's engineering project was "Opel." Notice the driveshaft with U-joints instead of Chevrolet's standard torque-tube design. *courtesy Noland Adams*

and in "running" fashion throughout the year, the easiest way to readily identify most 1954 models comes in back. Early in 1954 production, the short exhaust extensions used on all 1953 Corvettes were exchanged for longer tips, undoubtedly to help cure an exhaust staining problem that continually plagued the first Corvettes.

Yet another running change for 1954 came under the hood, where a different cam upped advertised output for the Blue Flame Six to 155 horsepower. Both 150- and 155-hp 1954 Corvettes were built. At some point along the line, engineers also traded the triple carburetors' three bullet-shaped air inlets for a more functional setup made up of two round air cleaners perched in conventional upright fashion. Most 1954 Corvettes also used a hood latch mechanism with only one interior release, while some early cars and all 1953 models featured two hood releases, one for each

latch. The Corvette frame differed slightly (concerning component mounting) in 1953 and 1954, as it also would in 1955.

That so little evidence was present to readily differentiate a 1953 Corvette from a 1954 was only right since Chevrolet officials themselves simply grouped them together under the same model year designation. And most witnesses at the time were none the wiser anyway since the 300 early cars were considerably slow in hitting the streets. On top of that, Chevrolet wasn't able to make an official press introduction until late September 1953 when journalists were invited to try out the new sports car at GM's Milford Proving Grounds in Michigan.

Chevrolet general manager Thomas Keating introduced the Corvette that day in an official press release: "In the Corvette we have built a sports car in the American tradition. It is not a racing car in the accepted sense that a European sports car is a race car. It is intended rather to satisfy the American public's conception of beauty, comfort and convenience, plus performance. Just as the American production sedan has become the criterion of luxury throughout the world, we have produced a superior sports car. We have not been forced to compromise with the driving and economic considerations that influence so broadly the European automotive design."

As a performance car, the new Corvette did well off the line by standards of the day. Top end

and handling qualities." Concluded the *R&T* report, "the Corvette corners flat like a genuine sports car should."

In the words of *Motor Trend's* Don MacDonald, "Chevrolet has produced a bucket-seat roadster that will hold its own with Europe's best, short of actual competition and a few imports that cost three times as much."

Nonetheless, could a sports car be a sports car without a clutch and a stick? Many felt not. In defense of the Corvette's Powerglide-only status, Mau-

A beautiful piece of art in itself, this mahogany body buck was used to make the first molds for the 1953 Corvette's fiberglass shell. *courtesy Noland Adams*

was just short of 110mph and reported acceleration figures were 11 seconds from zero to 60, 18 seconds for the quarter-mile. In the words of *Motor Life's* Hank Gamble, "the Corvette is a beauty—and it *goes!*"

But was it really a sports car? *Road & Track's* staffers asked that very question in their June 1954 issue. Overall, they "liked the Corvette very much," calling straight-line performance its most "outstanding characteristic." And in their opinion, "the second most outstanding characteristic of the Corvette is its really good combination of riding

rice Olley had earlier addressed the car's one apparently major disappointment.

"The use of an automatic transmission has been criticized by those who believe that sports car enthusiasts want nothing but a four-speed crash shift," explained Olley. "The answer is that the typical sports car enthusiast, like the 'average man,' or the square root of minus one, is an imaginary quantity. Also, as the sports car appeals to a wider and wider section of the public, the center of gravity of this theoretical individual is shifting from the austerity of the pioneer towards the luxury of modern

Chevrolet chief engineer Ed Cole (left) and division general manager Tom Keating take a quick look at the Corvette prototype sitting on its Motorama stage at New York's Waldorf-Astoria hotel in January 1953. Notice the unique fender trim and small push-button door handles—regular-production Corvettes from 1953-55 had no exterior door handles.

ideas." Concluded Olley, "there is no need to apologize for the performance of this car with its automatic transmission."

"That statement," wrote *R&T's* John Bond, "should get a rise from 100,000 *Road & Track* readers!"

Even more defensive was an official Chevrolet statement explaining that the division's new two-seater was "not intended to be used as a racing car." More than one journalist was quick to respond to this disclaimer.

"Definitely being discouraged is [the] competition use of the Corvette though its name means 'sloop of war,'" wrote Floyd Lawrence in *Motor Trend*. "This stands in marked contrast to foreign sports car producers who try to get their first models into the hands of well known racing drivers to insure a racing reputation for the car. It is reported that Briggs Cunningham's order for two Corvettes for possi-

ble entry in the Le Mans race was quietly turned down at headquarters."

Chevrolet officials were no dummies. They knew the Corvette wasn't anywhere near ready to race in 1953. Hell, it hadn't even gotten out of the blocks yet.

While Olley saw no need to apologize for the Powerglide, Chevy sales executives quickly discovered that many prospective customers were unable to forgive various other apparent pitfalls of the two-seat roadster. It seemed American car buyers didn't much care for the Corvette's pesky, leaky plexiglass side curtains and folding top. In reference to the clumsy top, MacDonald's *MT* report explained that apparently Chevy's "conception of the Corvette market is that no owner will be caught in the rain without a spare Cadillac."

Less troublesome but still a negative was the prospect of fumbling around for the interior door panel knob to gain entrance—remember, no exterior door handles. Cockpit instrumentation was also questioned. While gauges and a tachometer were included, they were located low in the center of the dashboard. The passenger basically had a better view of the 5000rpm tach—situated dead center in the dash—than the driver. All this helped explain why early Corvette sales never even came close to projections.

Then again, perhaps Chevrolet officials shot themselves in their own feet. Hoping to promote an exclusive image for their new Corvette, they initially limited availability of the first production run to "V.I.P." customers only. Most of the eager show-goers who saw the Motorama Corvette in January 1953 never even had a chance to touch a regular-production version. "If you've got an itch to get behind the wheel of a Chevrolet Corvette," wrote *MT's* Lawrence, "you might as well scratch it. Better are your chances of winning the Mille Miglia on a kiddie car." After explaining that the very few cars then available in the late summer of 1953 were going to General Motors executives, Lawrence quipped, "if [the] present distribution pattern continues, the hoped-for output of 300 units this year will scarcely take care of the top GM brass."

By the end of the year, only about 180 of the 300 1953 Corvettes built were sold as Chevrolet's sales geniuses couldn't find enough very important people willing to come to their by-invitation-only party. Much momentum had already been lost by the time the V.I.P-only qualification was dropped in the summer of 1954. As Don MacDonald explained in *Motor Trend*, "the long gap between initial publicity and availability has cooled the desires of many buyers." Meanwhile, the stockpile of unwanted Corvettes continued to grow as the St. Louis plant was rolling out 50 a day.

Alarmed by this unexpected apathetic trend, Chevrolet officials in June cut back production and halted fiberglass body panel construction entirely in Ohio. The St. Louis plant ended up building only 3,640 of the 10,000 Corvettes planned for 1954, and nearly a third of those were still sitting unsold as of January 1, 1955. Future prospects for continued production of America's only sport car looked bleak, helping explain why a mere 700 1955 Corvettes were built. Many atop GM's executive pecking order wanted to see Chevrolet cut its losses and quit the sports car game right there. But Ed Cole, Harley Earl and the rest wouldn't have it—somehow they were going to save this unique automobile from early extinction.

The first step towards salvation came early in 1955.

By then, nothing could be done about the car's cruder characteristics since the same body was back for a third year. The only notable changes again involved color choices, although some additional mystery surrounds what was actually offered. On the outside, Polo White was once more the

Chevrolet's first production Corvette rolled off the very short makeshift assembly line in Flint, Michigan, on June 30, 1953. Early models used standard Bel Air passenger car wheelcovers because the planned "knock-off" style covers weren't ready in time

Chevrolet didn't offer the comfort and convenience of a removable hardtop for the early Corvettes, but that didn't mean a fiberglass two-seater customer couldn't come in out of the rain. Various aftermarket companies started offering removable tops of their own not long after the Corvette was introduced. Chevrolet then took it upon itself to offer an optional detachable hardtop beginning in 1956.

paint of choice (representing nearly half of the 700 cars built), with Gypsy Red and the newly offered Harvest Gold making up the bulk of the remaining orders. Pennant Blue was apparently briefly carried over from 1954 then dropped in April 1955. Some sources say that Pennant Blue was then replaced by "Corvette Copper," while others list a "Coppertone Bronze." By either name, this latter shade was all but unknown in 1955.

Interior colors included red, dark beige, light beige, green and yellow, the latter two appropriately reserved for the yellowish Harvest Gold exte-

Chevrolet returned to GM's annual Motorama show circuit in 1954 with a bevy of Corvette dream cars. Appearing at top with the standard 1954 model is the fastback Corvair coupe. Below it is the passenger-line-based Nomad wagon, which led to a regular-production follow-up in 1955. In front is a hardtop 1954 Corvette with roll-up windows and exterior door handles.

rior paint. Top shades were also expanded, as white and dark green (again, for the Harvest Gold cars) joined beige.

The real news, however, came under the hood where overall impressions were boosted considerably thanks to the addition of Chevrolet's overhead-valve V-8, introduced that year to the delight of speed-conscious buyers in the low-priced field. From a passenger-line perspective, the new OHV V-8 had overnight transformed the old, reliable Chevy into the "Hot One."

With development dating back to just before Ed Cole came on board from Cadillac in 1952, Chevrolet's first modern V-8 displaced 265 cubic inches and featured a lightweight valvetrain using individual stamped steel rocker arms. These ball-stud rockers—an idea borrowed from Pontiac engineers—helped the short-stroke 265 wind up like nobody's business. In "Power Pack" trim under a 1955 Bel Air's hood, it produced 180hp at 4600rpm. Its potential beneath the Corvette's forward-hinged fiberglass lid was obvious.

Injecting more power into the Corvette equation had been tried before almost as soon as the car had hit the streets. More than one private V-8 swap had been performed. But the quickest, easiest way to add more horsepower was by bolting on one of McCulloch's centrifugal superchargers. The Paxton division of the McCulloch Company in California sold supercharger kits for many cars in the 1950s, and even supplied forced-induction blowers as factory-offered options through Kaiser (standard with 1954 Manhattans), Studebaker-Packard and Ford. When force feeding the Blue Flame six's three Carter carbs, a Paxton blower reportedly increased the Corvette's rear wheel horsepower by 35 percent, translating into a 0-60 time of about nine seconds.

Although impressive, the supercharged six-cylinder was still just a six, and a six still couldn't produce the image Cole and crew really wanted for the Corvette, especially after Ford began showing models of its upcoming Thunderbird early in 1954. A winner on looks alone, the planned two-seat "T-bird" would also be powered by a V-8, nothing less. Chevrolet had no choice but to respond accordingly.

Before Zora Arkus-Duntov came along to oversee Corvette performance, the man in charge of such development was three-time Indy 500 winner Mauri Rose, at far right. Here, he shows off the new V-8-equipped Corvette. *courtesy Michael Lamm*

The third experimental Corvette produced (notice the Motorama-style fender trim was later rebuilt as the prototype for the V-8 installation planned for 1955. This airborne moment came during chassis testing at GM's Milford Proving Grounds in May 1954. *courtesy Michael Lamm*

A prototype V-8 Corvette was undergoing testing as early as May 1954 under the direction of performance consultant and three-time Indy 500 winner Mauri Rose. Cole had hired Rose in August 1952 to oversee the division's performance parts development projects, a position Vince Piggins filled later in the 1950s. Rose's earliest challenges included developing the triple-carb setup for the Blue Flame six. Far more prominent was his involvement with the V-8-powered Corvette, a creation requiring not all that much sweat. Maurice Olley's X-member frame needed only a minor modification to allow clearance for the 265's fuel pump, and a bigger radiator with a fan shroud was added.

With a lumpier cam and a Carter four-barrel carburetor topped by a low-restriction chrome air cleaner, the Corvette's 265 V-8 was bumped up to 195 horsepower. Compression remained 8:1. Additional chrome dress-up appeared on the valve covers and the distributor's suppressive shielding. And a new 12-volt electrical system and automatic choke came along as part of the deal. On the outside, the V-8 Corvette was identified by the large gold "V" added to the "Corvette" script on each fender.

While some (as few as 10 perhaps) very early 1955 Corvettes were equipped with the 155hp Blue Flame six, the vast majority featured the high-winding 265 V-8. In turn, most of these cars also were equipped with the Powerglide automatic. A second transmission choice, the long-awaited three-speed manual, was introduced sometime during the year, apparently available only behind the Corvette's V-8 (no six-cylinder/auto trans cars are known). Estimates put three-speed Corvette production that year at probably 75.

As for more important numbers, according to *Road & Track*, the muscled-up V-8 Corvette couldn't be denied as far as sheer brute force was concerned. Rest to 60mph required a reasonably scant 8.7 seconds, with the far end of the quarter-mile showing up only 7.8 ticks later. The car's real-world top end was a tad short of 120mph, definitely impressive. "Loaded for bear" was *R&T's* description. As *Motor Life's* Ken Fermoyle saw it, "the V-8 engine makes this a far more interesting automobile and has upped performance to a point at least as good as anything in its price class."

Yet in other areas the Corvette was still lacking, whether from the perspective of a typical American customer looking for typical American conveniences or from the angle of sports car buffs who hoped to finally see a Yankee machine capable of putting Europeans in their place. Help in both cases was on the way.

Enter Zora Duntov.

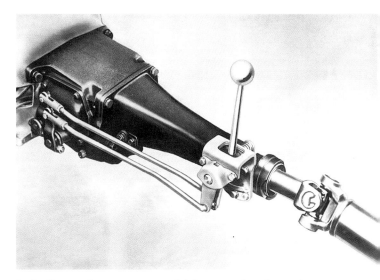

Easily the most common complaint concerning the early Corvettes involved its Powerglide-only status—an automatic transmission would never do if Chevrolet's two-seater was to ever take its place as a true sports car. That problem was solved late in 1955 production with the arrival of this three-speed manual transmission. *courtesy Noland Adams*

Chapter 3

1956-57
Off And Running

It easily ranks among the fastest stretches of sand in the world, an honor earned through both the various four-wheeled record runs once made there as well as the annual action still occurring today each spring when thousands of young, hormone-intensive collegiates hit these shores. For years, the Daytona area in Florida—roughly 25 miles of hard-packed, bullet-straight beaches—was home to high performance in America, beginning right after the turn of the century at Daytona's northern neighbor, Ormond Beach, the legendary "Birthplace of Speed."

There in April 1902, an Oldsmobile and a Winton both were clocked at a then-sizzling 57mph. Four years later, Fred Marriott's Stanley steamer hit 127mph, a word record, the first such international honor for the Ormond sands. Various other top end records followed, reaching 276mph in 1935 before speed freaks refocused their universe across the country to the Bonneville salt beds in Utah.

Florida's speed scene then shifted south to nearby Daytona Beach, where in March 1936, the area's first stock car race, sanctioned by the American Automobile Association (AAA), was run on a 3.2-mile course that led up the beach and down a closed-off section of the main coast road. In 1938, a young racer named Bill France took over promotion of the beach race, which that year became more than just an annual affair. Two races were run in 1938, three in 1939,

Exterior door handles, roll-up windows and optional two-tone paint schemes debuted along with a restyled fiberglass shell in 1956. Also notice the chromed headlight bezels—some early cars featured body-colored pieces.

and before France knew it he had a racing "season" in Florida. In December 1947, a France-led group voted to form the National Association of Stock Car Auto Racing. Nearly a half century later, NASCAR racing today is one of the sporting world's hottest tickets.

By 1956, Daytona Beach had again become the place to be in America for those with a need for speed. Along with the three annual beach races—Modified-Sportsman, Convertible class and Grand National—held in late February, the beach was also home to the various "Speed Weeks" performance trials for stock-class and modified-production factory cars, both foreign and domestic.

Domestic representatives that year included three specially prepared 1956 Corvettes. The trio arrived at Daytona Beach on a mission to prove that Chevrolet could indeed build a competitive sports car. Piloting the newly restyled two-seaters were two men and a woman, veteran racer John Fitch, aerobatic pilot Betty Skelton and a certain GM engineer named Zora Arkus-Duntov. For both Duntov and the car that had by then become "his baby," the 1956 Speed Weeks represented a "coming-out party" of sorts. By the time the sand settled, the man and his machine had grown forever entwined. And the Corvette's reputation as a real road rocket was born.

One of Zora Duntov's earliest jobs at GM engineering involved solving the exhaust staining problem on the tails of the early Corvettes. He proposed the twin exhaust tips be moved from the rear panel to the ends of the rear quarters for the 1955 model. The change, however, wasn't made until 1956.

An attractive, truly sporty three-spoke steering wheel helped spruce up the 1956 Corvette's interior, which carried over in similar fashion from the style used previously. A three-speed manual transmission was also standard in 1956, with the Powerglide now an $188.50 option.

Serving as the Corvette's chief engineer until his retirement in 1975, Zora Duntov commonly receives the lion's share of the credit for nearly every one of the fiberglass two-seater's advancements made during the 1950s and 1960s. Of course, he didn't do it all singlehandedly. But it was his experience, both as an engineer and a race driver, that was mainly responsible for the Corvette's kick start after 1955.

Duntov was born to Russian parents in Belgium on Christmas Day, 1909. By the time he was a teenager, he was demonstrating an intense interest for internal combustion machines. After studying mechanical engineering at universities in Leningrad and Germany, his thesis paper on supercharging was published in Berlin in 1934. A job designing superchargers then followed, as did various other engineering positions in Belgium and Paris. It was about this time that he also began toying with sports cars and racing. But both his engineering and racing careers were temporarily stalled with the coming of war in Europe.

Duntov and his family left France in December 1940 for the U.S., where he first worked as a consulting engineer. In 1942, he teamed up with his brother Yuri to open a machine shop in New York. This business soon became the Ardun Mechanical Corporation, the company title coming from a shortening of the *Arkus-Dun*tov name.

Six-cylinder power fell by the wayside after 1955. Top Corvette performance in 1956 came from a 265 V-8 with two Carter four-barrel carburetors. Advertised output was 225 horsepower. A single-carb 265, rated at 210hp, was also available, but few were installed. Various running changes made beneath the hood in 1956 included relocating the oil pan's dipstick to the driver's side of the engine. Early cars, like this one, had the dipstick on the passenger's side

One of three 1956 Corvettes specially prepared for the Daytona Beach Speed Weeks trials that year, this race-ready model was driven on the sands by aerobatic pilot Betty Skelton. Restored and owned today by noted Corvette collector Bill Tower, the Betty Skelton racer featured many speed-conscious modifications, including the addition of various aluminum trim pieces.

After the war, the Ardun company was contracted by Ford to help boost the power of Dearborn's old, reliable "flathead" V-8 for use in heavy-duty trucks. Zora then designed the legendary "Ardun head" overhead-valve conversion kit for Ford's valve-in-block flathead. These innovative aluminum cylinder heads featured hemispherical combustion chambers, centrally located spark plugs and inclined valves. But even though the Ardun heads did improve flathead performance considerably, Ford had already opted for the larger Lincoln V-8 for its trucks by the time Duntov's design was ready for market in 1949. Not all was lost, however, as Duntov heads then found their way into various Ford-powered race cars in the 1950s.

By far the biggest promoter of the Ardun-head V-8 was British sports car builder and racer Sydney Allard. He began offering the Ardun flathead engine in his J2 sports racer in 1949. Duntov himself went to work for Allard soon after, then returned to the States in late 1952 to work for Fairchild Aviation in Long Island, New York. Curiously, before he left England Duntov had contacted Chevrolet's Ed Cole about an engineering job, to no avail.

Then Zora saw the Corvette prototype at the Waldorf-Astoria in January 1953. "Now there's potential," he told *Hot Rod's* Jim McFarland in 1967. "I thought it wasn't a good car yet, but if you're going to do something, this looks good." Thus inspired, Duntov queried Cole's office a second time and was given a GM engineering position in May 1953. "Not for [the] Corvette or for anything of that sort," he told McFarland, "but for research and development and future stuff."

Nonetheless, it wasn't long before Duntov was tinkering with the Corvette chassis to improve overall handling. As he later explained, "this was not part of my normal assignment—just fiddling on the side." His first true Corvette assignment involved solving the exhaust staining problem in back, which he did by moving the twin tailpipe tips out to the farthest reach of each rear-quarter section. Considered then dropped for 1955, this design was incorporated the following year.

Duntov's involvement with the Corvette project then increased rapidly as first V-8 power was added and then additional chassis refinements were investigated. Finally in 1957, he was officially named Director of High Performance Vehicle Design and Development, with the Corvette, of course, being his top priority. America's only sports car would remain so for nearly two decades more.

As for the development of a better Corvette for 1956, it was Duntov's chassis experiments that paid off first. In his opinion, the early Corvette was a car with "two ends fighting each other" since considerable oversteer was designed in up front and almost as much roll understeer was inherent in back. All this was changed in 1956. As he wrote in *Auto Age*, "the target was to attain such handling characteristics that the driver of some ability could get really high performance safely. The main objects of suspension changes were: increase of high-speed stability, consistency in response to the steering wheel over a wide range of lateral accelerations and speeds, and improvement of power transmission on turns—that is, [the] reduction of unloading of [the] inside rear wheels."

These goals were accomplished by adjusting suspension geometry. Front suspension location was changed by adding shims where the front cross-member attached to the frame, a move that increased caster angle. Roll oversteer was also minimized by changing the steering's main idler arm angle, again by shims. In back, roll understeer was reduced by revamping the leaf spring hangers to lessen the slope of the springs.

Weight distribution was improved as well ever so slightly (by 1 percentage point) to 52 percent front, 48 percent rear, since the 265ci V-8, at 531 pounds, weighed 41 pounds less than the big Blue Flame six. And power was boosted considerably thanks to the addition of a second Carter four-barrel carburetor to the 265's induction setup.

Initially, two power choices were offered for 1956, the twin-carb 265, with 225 healthy horses, and a 210hp version with its single Carter four-barrel. Both engines featured a compression in-

Beneath the Betty Skelton beach racer were special brakes fitted with finned drums, vented backing plates and special cooling ducts. Although not available for regular-production Corvettes in 1956, this type of equipment would become an official option the following year.

crease to 9.25:1. Some confusion still exists over which of these powerplants was actually standard, although the lower performance 210hp 265 has been logically listed as such over the years. The dual-four V-8, however, was apparently the first powerplant offered beneath a 1956 Corvette's hood. As for this engine's regular production option (RPO) number, 469, that came later in the run after the 210hp engine reportedly appeared on the scene to replace its twin-carb counterpart as base equipment.

Some evidence to this move came early that summer via a *Road & Track* road test. In reference to the 225hp V-8's tendency for "'flatness' of carburetion on take-off," that report explained that "this appears to be a characteristic of the two four-barrel carburetors and possibly accounts for the change to a single four-barrel carburetor as standard equipment (210bhp)." According to official Chevrolet paperwork dated May 28, 1956, the 225hp 265 was about that time first listed as an option and

Famed Daytona Beach speed merchant Smokey Yunick did the prep work on the three 1956 Corvette beach racers. On Skelton's car, he reportedly installed a four-speed manual transmission, equipment that wouldn't be available to Corvette buyers until 1957. Yunick also added his trademark cool-air induction system, which drew in the denser, outside atmosphere from near the passenger's side headlight and delivered it via ductwork to the twin carbs. That setup has long since disappeared, although a small intake grille (not visible here) still exists at the right front corner of the engine compartment.

given the appropriate code, RPO 469. Oddly, this apparent switch is also marked by various trivial mechanical changes to the dual-carb V-8, including relocating the oil dipstick from the right side of the engine to the left. Coincidentally, the vast majority of the 3,467 1956 Corvettes built featured the 225hp 265. Very few 210-horse examples are known.

Whatever the engine choice, a base Corvette in 1956 did come equipped with an honest-to-good-

ness manual transmission, the same three-speed box briefly offered late in 1955. Gear ratios were 2.21:1, first, 1.31:1, second. Those who preferred shiftless driving could still have the two-speed Powerglide automatic, listed under RPO 313. Reportedly, installation totals of the two transmissions were split roughly right down the middle.

Again using 11-inch drums, the brake system basically carried over, save for new linings that were more fade resistant and wore longer. Standard axle ratio in 1956 was again 3.55:1, with a 3.27:1 differential listed as an option under RPO 471.

Truly new was the fresh, modern-looking body that went atop that revamped chassis in 1956. This restyle was quick to impress as both a marked improvement on what came before as well as a faithfully updated rendition of the original image. While the toothy grille up front helped remind onlookers that the 1956 model was indeed a Corvette, the more conventionally located headlights and recessed taillights gave the car more of an impression of forward motion.

Complementing those speedier-looking lines were twin "windsplits" on the hood and scalloped "cove" panels behind each front wheel opening. These coves could remain the same overall body color or could be painted a contrasting shade—the optional two-tone finish was a Corvette first. Solid color choices numbered six in 1956; Onyx Black, Aztec Copper, Cascade Green, Arctic Blue, Venetian Red, and Polo White. Priced at $19.40, the RPO 440 two-tone combination was also available in six forms. Interior trim shades were two, red and beige, while three folding top colors (depending on paint choice) were offered, black, white and beige.

Additional exterior firsts included the two simulated scoops added atop each front fender, items reminiscent of the 1953 Motorama prototype. Completing the exterior remake were new knock-off wheelcovers that amazingly carried over in nearly identical fashion up through 1962. In 1959, this design was modified with 10 rectangular slots added to help cool the brakes.

On the street, the restyled, muscled-up Corvette looked every bit as fast as it ran. According to *Road & Track*, that amounted to 0-60 in 7.3 seconds, 15.8 seconds for the quarter-mile, this in a three-speed model. Performance for its Powerglide-equipped counterpart was listed as 8.9 and 16.5 seconds, respectively. Nice numbers either way. *Sports Car Illustrated's* Roger Huntington thought so. He called the 1956 Corvette's 225hp V-8 "one of the hottest production engines in the world—regardless of piston displacement." And to think Duntov wasn't even done yet.

Both he and Cole, who would be promoted to Chevrolet general manager that July, wanted the world to know just how fast the revamped

Corvette had become by 1956. Zora was confident he could squeeze 150mph out of the car with some additional work. Cole quickly gave the go-ahead for that effort with the goal being a trip south to Florida to show off the results during the aforementioned Speed Weeks trials.

It was then that Zora developed the aptly named "Duntov cam," a potent solid-lifter bumpstick that really brought the little 265 V-8 to life. While lift was a bit less than Chevrolet's existing top performance V-8 cam, the Duntov cam's duration for both intake and exhaust was considerably longer. Found under RPO 448 or 449, depending on your source, the "Special High-Lift Camshaft" was only available for the 225hp RPO 469 V-8. Output for the Duntov-cam RPO 469 engine, although not officially listed, was commonly put at 240 horsepower. Chevrolet paperwork recommended that this combination only be used "for racing purposes only."

Duntov, Fitch and Skelton showed why on the sands of Daytona in late February 1956. For Skelton, an experienced pilot, test driver and corporate spokesperson who then worked for Campbell-Ewald, Chevrolet's ad agency, a day at the beach would never mean the same again. As she later told *Road & Track's* Andrew Bornhop, "it was very exciting because when the tide would go out it would leave these little puddles of water. And after the cars ran a few times through the measured mile, these pools would become deep ruts that would get you airborne. That was kind of fun. It was just a marvelous time, driving on the beach and being there in the early days of Corvettes with all those great people. It was such an honor to be part of the activity. And, of course, the Corvette was the star of the show."

Star, indeed. Duntov's prediction rang true as he drove one of the cars to a top two-way average speed of 150.533mph. Fitch's Corvette hit 145.543mph, while Skelton turned in a 137.773mph average. Without a doubt, the Corvette had arrived.

Then, just as quickly, it was off again, this time farther south to Sebring, Florida, home of the 12-hour endurance race that each spring brought the world's best sports-racing machines to America.

Raced at various venues in the years after its February 1956 appearance at Daytona Beach, Betty Skelton's Corvette was fitted with a rollbar somewhere along the line. The small windscreen was used at Daytona. Notice the tachometer, relocated on the steering column where it belonged. A plate covers the stock tach location in the center of the dash.

A bore job boosted displacement for Chevrolet's high-winding V-8 to 283 cubic inches in 1957. Two dual-carb 283s were offered that year, the hydraulic-cam 245hp version and this brute, the 270hp variety with its solid-lifter "Duntov cam."

After kicking up some sand on the beach, Chevrolet's Corvette showed up a month later in Sebring to hopefully show everyone it could do more than just go fast in a straight line. Duntov declined to take part this time, so it was up to John Fitch to lead the four-car Sebring team on March 24, 1956.

On the surface, Chevrolet officials did everything they could to distance themselves publicly from Fitch's four-car team, which was "fronted" through Dick Doane's Raceway Enterprises in Dundee, Illinois. All theatrics aside, the effort was definitely fully factory backed, right down to the engineering advancements hiding beneath the skins of each car. Springs and shocks were heavy-duty and

One more color choice, Inca Silver, was added for the 1957 Corvette, which basically carried over unchanged at a glance from the outside. This Cascade Green 1957, one of 550 Corvettes painted that color in 1957, is equipped with the 270hp 283cid V-8, RPO 469C. Price for RPO 469C was $182.95. Production was 1,621.

A four-speed stick was introduced as a Corvette option, RPO 685, in 1957. Priced at $188.30, this close-ratio gearbox was snapped up by 664 buyers that year.

brakes featured finned drums with wider shoes wearing sintered cerametallix linings. Three of the cars relied on the twin-carb 265 backed by the standard three-speed. The fourth featured an enlarged 307ci V-8 with 10.2:1 compression and headers. Behind this 275hp beast was a German-built ZF four-speed transmission. All four cars rolled on Halibrand knock-off magnesium wheels.

Painted white with blue stripes and coves, the team Corvettes were not easily missed at Sebring—for more than one reason. "The crowds watched half curiously, half mockingly as the Chevys lumbered around the tricky circuit turning practice laps," wrote Al Kidd, sports editor for *Motor Trend*. "The same Corvettes which had looked so low and racy to them around their home towns were hulking monsters compared to the nimble competition. Just about everyone wondered what in the world the Corvettes were doing there in such fast company, and some of the Chevrolet Division officials on hand weren't quite sure themselves."

Those officials had a fair idea after 12 hours of racing around the rough-and-tough 5.2-mile course. While two of the production cars fell out of the race—along with 35 rivals—the modified Corvette, driven by Fitch and Walt Hansgen, finished ninth overall and tops in its class with an average speed less than 8mph slower than the win-

Hands down, the most important addition to the Corvette package in 1957 was Ramjet fuel injection, an optional induction system that put America's only sports car into an entirely different league as far as performance was concerned. Fuel injection would remain the top Corvette performance option up through 1965.

ning Ferrari's 84mph clocking. The other "team" car finished 15th. Yet another Corvette, this one definitely a private entry, completed the race in 23rd, second from last.

Simply finishing at Sebring, however, represented a reasonably meritorious achievement, a fact not lost on Campbell-Ewald. Almost immediately, a magazine ad appeared featuring one of the Sebring Corvettes in the pits under the heading, "The Real McCoy." That ad described the 1956 Corvette as "a tough, road-gripping, torpedo-on-wheels with the stamina to last through the brutal 12 hours of Sebring." As for more innocent bystanders, most of them were also impressed, however humbly, by the Corvette's gutsy first-time effort in international competition. "The Corvette was once a joke at serious races," announced Kidd, "now it's a grudgingly respected underdog. What kind of a future can it have in such fast company?"

While that question remained then unanswered, the Corvette's future on the street appeared particularly bright once the new 1956 model ap-

Supplied by Rochester, the Corvette's Ramjet "fuelie" setup went atop two very different 283 V-8s in 1957. The milder, hydraulic-cam version was rated at 250 horses. With the Duntov cam inside, the injected 283 was rated at 283hp, making it the second American car to offer one horsepower per cubic inch of displacement—Chrysler had been the first the previous year.

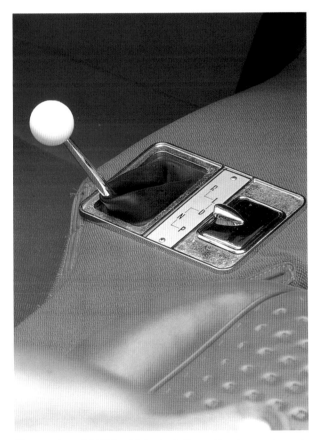

The topless 1957 fuel-injected Corvette shown here is equipped with the 250hp Ramjet-equipped 283 backed by a Powerglide automatic transmission, a package listed under RPO 579C that year. Only 102 RPO 579C 1957 Corvettes were built. Another 182 featured RPO 579A, which consisted of the 250hp fuelie V-8 and a manual transmission.

peared. Prospective customers who previously had been turned off the by the less amiable characteristics of the early Corvettes had next to nothing to complain about in 1956.

Fiberglass firsts from a convenience standpoint that year included real side windows that actually rolled up and down, exterior door handles, an adjustable seat for the passenger, and a fresh-air heater instead of the previously used recirculating unit. Additional newfangled features came on the options list, including power windows (RPO 426) and hydraulic operation for the folding convertible roof (RPO 473). Seat belts also appeared for the first time, albeit as dealer-installed equipment. But topping everything was the new removable hardtop, a stylish, fully functional option that added both class and convenience.

Removable hardtops had appeared for the Corvette in 1954 and 1955 thanks to various aftermarket companies. As a factory option (RPO 419) in 1956, Chevrolet's removable top could have been added at no cost in place of the standard folding soft top or as an accompaniment along with the nylon top for $188.30. The former installation was chosen by 629 buyers, the latter by 1,447 others. All were probably tickled pink about the way that top kept wetness away.

Was it any wonder Corvette sales jumped 400 percent in 1956?

Yet another major leap came in 1957 when Chevrolet sold 6,339 Corvettes, nearly twice as many as in the previous year. Having redeemed itself, Chevrolet's fiberglass two-seater was finally off and running as public confidence in the concept took root. Not much more than a cute curiosity in 1953-55, the Corvette had overnight been transformed into a real sexpot. So much so, customers apparently couldn't care less that the 1957 model was essentially a carbon copy of the 1956. At a glance, that is.

The quickest way to identify a rare Airbox Corvette without opening the hood comes inside, where the tachometer was relocated from the dash to the steering column. A round plate then went in place of the opening left in the center of the dash.

Beneath the skin was another story.

First and foremost was the 1957 Corvette's "new" engine, a bored-out version of the proven 265 V-8. Now displacing 283 cubic inches with 9.5:1 compression, the 1957 V-8 was rated at 220 horsepower in standard form with a single Carter four-barrel. The dual-four option was again available in two forms, this time identified as RPOs 469A and 469C. RPO 469A added twin Carter carbs and a hydraulic cam, while 469C used the mechanical Duntov cam. Advertised output for RPO 469A was 245hp at 5000rpm, while its solid-lifter brother produced 270hp at 6000 revs. The standard transmission was again a three-speed manual, with the Powerglide automatic available optionally at the same price listed in 1956.

The performance boost supplied by the 270hp 283 was more than enough to bring 'em running into Chevrolet dealerships. A *Sport Car Illustrated* road test (using a three-speed model with 3.55:1 gears) produced a scintillating 0-60 pass of only 6.8 seconds. Quarter-mile performance was 15.0 seconds at 95mph, while top end reached 123mph. But wait, there was more.

A whole host of hot performance options were introduced for Corvette customers in 1957, a few of them coming along a bit after the new cars themselves debuted in the fall of 1956. Priced at $188.30, RPO 685, a four-speed manual transmission, was released on April 9, 1957. The Chevrolet-designed, Borg-Warner-built T-10 four-speed featured gear ratios of 2.20:1, first; 1.66:1, second; and 1.31:1, third. According to a Chevrolet press release, "the four forward speeds of the new transmission are synchronized to provide a swift and smooth response. The close-ratio gears also permit easy downshift to make maximum use of the engine for braking as an added safety factor."

"When you can whip the stick around from one gear to any other the way you'd stir a can of paint, that's a gearbox that's synchronized," responded Walt Woron in the September 1957 issue of *Motor Trend*. "And when you can downshift from second to first at 40mph without double clutching, that's slightly more than just an 'easy downshift.'" Corvette buyers snatched up 664 four-speeds that first year.

But easily the most impressive new option for 1957 was an innovative induction system for the 283 V-8. Wearing a definitely heavy price tag of $484.20, the legendary "Ramjet" fuel injection setup was offered for the first time that year to Corvette customers and passenger car buyers alike. Its roots went back to development work by engineer John Dolza. Early in 1955, Ed Cole also put Zora Duntov on the Dolza project, which quickly escalated. A prototype fuel injection installation was being tested on a Chevrolet V-8 by the end of the year. And not even a 1956 test track crash that put Duntov in a body cast could keep him from finalizing the de-

Feeding cooler, denser air to the 283hp 283 fuelie beneath an Airbox Corvette's hood was a special plenum box (at top just to right of master cylinder) mounted to the driver's side inner fender panel. Ductwork at the front of that box drew outside air from the left of the radiator; additional ductwork led from the filter inside the plenum box to the Rochester injection unit.

sign, which was being readied almost right up to the date the new 1957 Corvettes were introduced.

The Rochester Products-built "fuelie" system did typical carburetors one better by, among other things, eliminating flooding and fuel starvation caused when hard turns sent the gas supply in the carb bowl centrifuging off sideways away from the pickup. This latter problem in particular had worked against the dual-carb racing Corvettes at Sebring in March 1956.

In place of those carbs, the Ramjet system not only delivered fuel more evenly in a much more efficient manner, it did so instantly. Throttle response for the fuel-injected Corvette was superb. In *Road & Track's* words, "the fuel injection engine is an absolute jewel, quiet and remarkably docile when driven gently around town, yet instantly transformable into a roaring brute when pushed hard."

Various problems, however, plagued the early fuelie cars, the most prominent one involving hard starts. Uninformed owners didn't help matters during starting by typically pumping the accelerator, a definite no-no. Once hot, the fuelie engine simply refused completely. While these starting maladies were soon minimized, the Ramjet unit remained

Special brake and suspension features like those used at Daytona and Sebring in the spring of 1956 became Corvette options in 1957. This is the rear wheel assembly included in RPO 684, the heavy-duty racing suspension package. Finned drums and an intricate brake cooling duct setup (notice the air inlet scoop above the leaf spring at the front of the backing plate) were part of RPO 684, as were various beefed suspension components.

This styling studio clay model shows the 1956 Corvette shape to come, minus the scoops that returned atop each fender after first appearing on the Motorama prototype of January 1953. Notice the body-colored headlight bezels. *courtesy Noland Adams*

Zora Duntov at the wheel of the 1956 Corvette he took to Daytona Beach, Florida, in February 1956. There, he topped 150mph during speed tests. To the left is Betty Skelton; to the right is the rear wheel of John Fitch's Corvette. *courtesy Bill Tower*

Discounting a few minor changes, most made as part of the switch from six-cylinder power to V-8, the Corvette's chassis remained quite similar to its 1953-55 predecessor. The most apparent change here is the new dual-carb 265 V-8.

finicky when it came to keeping it in "proper tune." And compounding this situation over the years was the plain fact that so few typical garages were prepared to service this rarely seen equipment. More than one owner of an early fuelie Corvette gave up entirely and exchanged the Ramjet setup for the more conventional carburetor, even though in some cases the frustrations encountered were the result of unrelated problems mistakenly blamed on the fuel injection equipment.

In its first year, that equipment was available in various forms, all listed under RPO 579. RPOs 579A and 579C both featured the hydraulic-cam 250hp 283 fuelie, the former including a manual transmission, the latter the Powerglide automatic. RPO 579B was the fabled 283hp 283 F.I. V-8, a certified screamer with 10.5:1 compression, the solid-lifter Duntov cam and a manual trans only. Chevrolet promotional people have long loved to claim that this engine was Detroit's first to reach the magical one-horsepower-per-cubic-inch barrier. But they have also long overlooked Chrysler's 300B of 1956, which could've been equipped with an optional 355hp 354ci "hemi" V-8. Production of the 283hp fuelie in 1957 was 713. Another 284 250hp versions were built, 182 manual transmission cars, 102 automatics.

Performance for the top fuelie Corvette was simply stunning. *Road & Track's* testers managed 0-

Veteran American race driver John Fitch went along with Duntov and Skelton to Daytona in 1956 to prove just how high the new Corvette could fly. After the 1956 Speed Weeks trials, he then took another Corvette team to Sebring to test the car up against live competition from Europe. *courtesy Bill Tower*

60 in just 5.7 seconds and the quarter-mile in 14.3; excellent results even for today, totally outrageous nearly 40 years ago. Published top end for the "283/283" Corvette was 132mph.

Yet another version of the 283/283 fuelie was offered in 1957, this one clearly built with competition in mind. One of the lessons learned during the high-speed runs at Daytona and Sebring in 1956 was the value of allowing cooler, denser outside air entry into an engine's induction system, as opposed to simply letting it breathe in the hot underhood atmosphere. Experimentation with "cold-air" induction setups led to the creation of the so-called "Airbox" Corvette.

The idea was simple. A plenum box was fabricated and mounted on the driver's side fenderwell panel. Up front, this box led to an opening in the support bulkhead beside the radiator where outside air could be "rammed" into it. Inside the box was an air filter; connected to the box's side was a rubberized duct sealing that filter to the Ramjet injection unit. All this added up to a few more ponies as the airbox Corvette's injected 283 breathed in its denser supply of precious oxygen. The Airbox option was listed as RPO 579E, priced at $726.30. Only 43 579E 1957 Corvettes were built, bringing total fuelie production that year to 1,040.

Additional Airbox modifications included moving the tachometer from its less-than-desirable stock spot in the center of the dash to atop the steering column where it could do its job like it should. The old tach location opening in the dash was then

Along with being a treat to the eyes, Betty Skelton was an accomplished pilot and record-setting driver. She also served as an advertising spokesperson for both Dodge and Chevrolet. *courtesy Bill Tower*

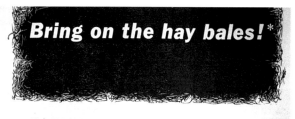

Campbell-Ewald, Chevrolet's advertising agency and Betty
Skelton's employer, wasted little time after the record-setting runs at Daytona in February 1956. The Corvette had arrived as a true competitor, at least in Yankee terms.

covered by a round plate. And since Airbox Corvettes
were meant for racing, both a radio and heater were
not available. Coincidentally, with the a radio not
present, ignition shielding wasn't required. This in
turn meant plug wires could be run more directly
from the distributor to the spark plugs over the valve
covers as far away from the hot exhaust manifolds as
possible. Plug wires on all other 1957 Corvettes were
routed the long way down along the cylinder heads
below the manifolds since this was the easiest place to
mount the static-suppressive shielding.

The Airbox equipment wasn't the only
new-for-1957 performance option inspired by earlier racing activities. A Positraction differential
and wide 15x5.5 wheels were also introduced that
year. Three different "Posi" rearends were available, RPO 677 with a 3.70:1 ratio, 678 with 4.11:1
gears, and the stump-pulling 679 with 4.56:1
cogs. The steel wheels, RPO 276, were a half-inch
wider than stock rims and came only with a
small, plain hubcap in place of the standard, ornate "knock-off" wheelcover.

A heavy-duty suspension option, listed under
RPO 581, also entered the fray early on. Included
were beefed springs front and rear; larger, stiffer
shocks; a thicker front stabilizer bar; and a quick
steering adapter. Sometime early in the 1957 model
run, this option was repackaged under RPO 684 as a

heavy-duty brake package was added along with the
suspension components.

Sounding very much like the equipment list
found on the four Sebring Corvettes of 1956, the
RPO 684 brakes featured cerametallix linings, finned
drums, and vented backing plates with scoops to
catch cooling air. Helping deliver this air to the rear
wheel scoops was a somewhat odd ductwork
arrangement that began at each side of the radiator,
ran back through the engine compartment, down
around each front wheelwell to inside the lower
rocker panels. At the trailing end of each rocker was
was a short, fiberglass deflector duct that directed
the airflow inboard towards the scoops on each
vented backing plate.

Mounting this extensive ductwork meant a
few additional changes were required. The horn re-
lay had to be relocated beneath the hood and apparently modified mounting plates were needed in
back for the heavy-duty shock absorbers.

A Positraction rearend was mandatory along
with RPO 684, which itself was only available with
the 270- and 283-horse engines. Its price was

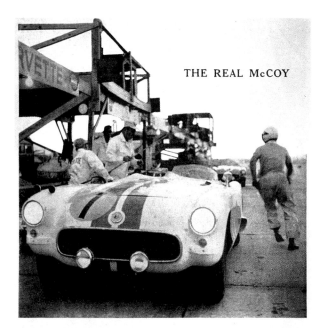

One month after Duntov's three-car team kicked up the sands
at Daytona, a second group went farther south to Sebring,
Florida, to compete in the annual 12-hour endurance race.
And again, a popular ad campaign resulted.

In 1957, a Corvette team returned to Sebring, this time with a production-car effort (foreground) and the all-out SS (car number 1). Bill Mitchell's 1956 SR-2 also competed that year.

Along with fuel injection, Corvette buyers were also treated to an optional four-speed manual transmission in 1957.

$780.10. Only 51 1957 Corvettes were built with this Sebring-inspired performance package.

Apparently armed to the teeth, Chevrolet's Corvette returned to Daytona Beach in February 1957, this time taking top standing-start mile honors in the production class as Paul Goldsmith's fiberglass two-seater ran 91.301mph. And in March, two 1957 airbox Corvettes equipped with all the goodies—four-speed and RPO 684—took to the starting grid at Sebring, where they were joined for the annual 12-hour enduro by Bill Mitchell's SR-2 (see chapter four) and Duntov's SS (see chapter five).

While the ill-fated SS dropped out early, the SR-2 soldiered on, and finished 16th. As for the production cars (which, by the way, ran with their airboxes removed), one finished one place ahead of the SR-2, the other managed to come in 12th and win its class—yet another public relations feather for caps of Ed Cole and crew.

By 1957, the Corvette had, at least from an American perspective, established itself as a top performing grand tourer. As *Road & Track* explained it, "Chevrolet said, back in 1954, that they were in the sports car business to stay, and their competition successes of the past two years certainly show that they mean it."

While those successes would continue, they were basically limited to SCCA competition on these shores. After driving a Corvette to an SCCA C/Production national title in 1956, Dr. Dick Thompson, the "Flying Dentist" from Washington D.C., won another SCCA title (B/Production) in a Corvette in 1957. That same year, J. E. Rose piloted his Corvette to the SCCA's B/Sports-Racing crown. This was just the beginning as Corvettes would go on to dominate SCCA competition throughout the 1950s.

But most hopes—primarily fostered by Duntov—to take the Corvette to international racing heights were all but dashed that summer when the Automobile Manufacturers Association stepped in. Alarmed by Detroit's escalating "horsepower race," the AMA board issued the following decree in June 1957:

"Whereas, the Automobile Manufacturers Association believes that automobile manufacturers should encourage owners and drivers to evaluate passenger cars in terms of useful power and ability to provide safe, reliable, and comfortable transportation, rather than in terms of capacity for speed. Now therefore, this board unanimously recommends to the member companies engaged in the manufacture and sale of passenger cars that they:

"Not participate or engage in any public contest, competitive event or test of passenger cars involving or suggesting racing or speed, including acceleration tests, or encourage or furnish financial, engineering, manufacturing, advertising, or public relations assistance, or supply 'pace cars' or 'official cars,' in connection with any such contest, event, or test, directly or indirectly.

"Nor participate or engage in, or encourage or assist employees, dealers, or others in the advertising or publicizing of (a) any race or speed contest, test, or competitive event involving or suggesting speed, whether public or private, involving passenger cars or the results thereof; or (b) the actual or comparative capabilities of passenger cars for speed, or the specific engine size, torque, horsepow-

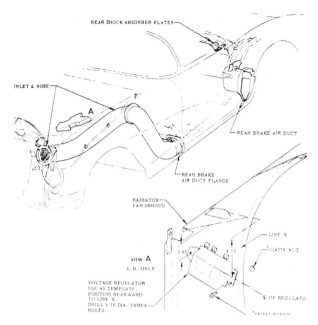

Long ducts ran down both sides of 1957 Corvettes equipped with RPO 684, the racing suspension package. These ducts took cooling air in from behind the headlights and directed it, via the rocker panels, into the scoop on each rear backing plate.

er or ability to accelerate or perform in any context that suggests speed."

With the AMA "ban" in place, Chevrolet was forced by GM's upper office to cease and desist as far as shenanigans like the Corvette SS project and the Sebring racing efforts were concerned. While much clandestine factory support of competition Corvettes continued, and performance developments were by no means derailed, one can only wonder what might've resulted had Cole, Duntov and the rest been allowed to keep up the pace set in 1956 and early 1957.

They didn't do a bad job after 1957 as it was. Even with the AMA raining on Chevrolet's parade, the Corvette continued rolling on as America's only sports car.

Chapter 4

Executive Privileges
1956 Corvette SR-2

Chevrolet people had grown duly excited about their Corvette by the summer of 1956. Nearly put on ice a year or so before, Chevy's fiberglass two-seater had almost overnight been transformed from an average-performing curiosity into a sizzling sporting machine. First came V-8 power in 1955, followed by a totally fresh, certainly sexy body the following year. And if prospective Corvette customers still weren't sure about just how hot America's only sports car had become, they only needed to watch Zora Duntov, John Fitch and Betty Skelton during their high-flying record runs down Daytona Beach in February 1956. After Fitch's trip to Sebring that March, it was time to "bring on the hay bales"—the Corvette was now an honest-to-goodness race car.

These were high times indeed. As Bill Mitchell, then Harley Earl's righthand man at GM Styling, later wrote in 1984, "the 1954 Corvette looked great, but was a weak performer. Its six-cylinder engine was not exactly what you would expect in a sleek-looking sports car. Fortunately, along came the V-8 and Zora and we beat some Jags and Mercedes at Elkhart Lake and Watkins Glen, and when that happened, boy, the Corvette became something! We were really inspired then."

Mitchell was especially inspired when it came to the Corvette, which in his words would become "my baby" once he replaced Earl at the top of GM

Chevrolet built three SR-2 Corvettes in 1956, this one for styling executive Bill Mitchell. Mitchell's car, like the first SR-2 built for Harley Earl's son Jerry, were race cars. The third, built for GM president Harlow Curtice, was a street-going showboat.

Bill Mitchell's SR-2 was the first "high-fin" car; when originally built, Jerry Earl's SR-2 featured a much small, symmetrical "low fin" on its decklid, as would the SR-2 built for Harlow Curtice.

Styling following Harley's retirement in 1958. Mitchell also loved racing, as ably demonstrated by the 1959 Stingray, his so-called "private" race car that won a Sports Car Club of America (SCCA) championship in 1960 piloted by Dr. Dick Thompson. Based on the chassis of the 1957 SS "Mule," Mitchell's Stingray foretold much of the all-new classic Corvette look that would debut for 1963 wearing the same name, only spelled "Sting Ray."

Without a doubt, Mitchell's Stingray racer was a "privateer" in name alone, a ruse carried out to help innocent, hopefully naive bystanders believe

Chevrolet was still adhering 100 percent to the Automobile Manufacturers Association's "ban" on factory racing involvement set down in 1957. Thompson, the legendary "Flying Dentist," was also commonly referred to as an independent racer, even though the backdoor to Chevrolet Engineering was always left wide open for him.

Such shenanigans had not been needed in 1956 when Mitchell asked Chevrolet designers to create his first personal Corvette racer, the SR-2. And he wasn't the only top GM officer to take advantage of executive privileges that year. Two other SR-2

Corvettes were built in 1956, one by request of Harley Earl, the other for GM president Harlow "Red" Curtice. Like Mitchell's, Earl's SR-2 was built for racing, while Curtice's was a street car. And like so many of the special Corvette racers and experimental machines created over the years, all three SR-2s are still around today to help demonstrate just how privileged GM execs were some four decades ago.

Clearly those were different times, a "more personal" era when a corporate heavy hitter could easily throw his weight around with his own interests in mind. This is exactly what GM vice president Harley Earl did when son Jerry decided to go racing in 1956. The younger Earl's first choice for track duty was a Ferrari, a decision that didn't exactly make father proud. It seemed Jerry Earl wasn't all that impressed with the restyled Corvette, even with its new dual-carb V-8 injecting more optional horsepower into the equation. Nonetheless, Harley Earl wasn't about to let his son campaign an Italian exotic instead of Detroit iron. Or Detroit fiberglass.

The elder Earl's solution to the problem was simple. "Jerry," he probably asked, "what if I had my people build you a custom-bodied Corvette race car using all those wonderful chassis modifications track tested at Sebring in March by John Fitch's competition Corvette team?" Maybe he didn't ask. After all, Mr. Earl was a very big man. Either way, Jerry Earl did agree to the deal. And just like that, the first SR-2 Corvette was born.

Explaining the car's name is simple enough. Inside Chevrolet Engineering, the special performance components created for the Corvettes that had scorched the sands at Daytona and competed valiantly at Sebring early in 1956 were known by an "SR" designation, a reference to either "Special Racer," "Sports Racing" or "Sebring Racer," depending on your source. Mixed messages aside, those early Corvette factory racers were the first SR models. Logically, any purpose-built racing machines to follow would wear the name "SR-2."

SR-2 production began with Jerry Earl purchasing a new 1956 Corvette, serial number E56F002522, off the showroom floor at Ray White Chevrolet in Grosse Point, Michigan. In early May, the car went into GM Styling, under shop order number 90090, where the body was hastily modified and the chassis beefed up. Amazingly, the completed SR-2 rolled out less than four weeks later, leading some to conclude that the reworked shell was simply dropped atop an existing race-ready chassis from one of Fitch's Sebring racers. Just like the Fitch cars, Earl's SR-2 featured quick steering, stiffer springs and shocks, a limited-slip differential, and bigger brakes with sintered cerametallix linings, finned drums and special cooling "scoops" mounted on vented backing plates. Halibrand knock-off wheels were also used. Dual exhaust pipes dumped

out, in typical race car fashion, directly in front of each rear wheel.

The modified metallic blue fiberglass shell that went on top featured an extended nose and a somewhat peculiar—albeit small—tailfin protruding from the center of the decklid. The stock windshield was replaced by two small windscreens, while the interior was dressed up to a far greater degree than your average race car. Footwells remained carpeted with padded vinyl inserts on each side. Vinyl covered the transmission tunnel, which was topped with a chrome-plated fire extinguisher. Along with the original-equipment power window lifts, the car's stock seats were retained, but were re-upholstered in blue vinyl. Extra instrumentation included a tachometer on the steering column and gauges mounted in a stainless steel panel located in the center of the dash. Oddly, a radio was initially present, although no antenna was noticeable. Completing the interior makeover was a wood-rimmed steering wheel.

Back on the outside, large turn signal lamps were added beneath the headlights, and a series of louvers were formed into the hood to help keep engine compartment temperatures within reason. Cooling was the also the goal behind the rather ornate scoops incorporated into the bodyside cove panels on both doors. Although these bright baubles did look like nothing more than typical styling tricks, they were fully functional.

Each scoop directed air flow into internal ductwork that ran back out the door's trailing edge through a seal in the doorjam into another duct in the body. From there, flow was channeled into the rear wheelhouse where it was aimed at the cooling scoop attached to the leading edge of the brake drum's backing plate. Hopefully, the precious outside air then entered the backing plates through vents and made its way inside the drum to help bring down internal temperatures. Simple, right?

While the functional aspects of the SR-2 body modifications were top priority—remember, this was a race car—the aesthetic end results proved to be every bit as successful. Most critics of the day loved everything about the SR-2 look, including that little fin in back. As *Motor Life's* Art Dean saw it, "[this] custom Corvette from the factory could be the forecast of things to come from Chevrolet, and if it is, they've got a winner." The one forecast the SR-2 did make involved its louvered hood, which eventually resurfaced—in nonfunctional form—as a production Corvette feature for 1958 only.

Telling the 1956 SR-2 tale from a power perspective also involves a little forecasting. Today, all three cars feature fuel injection and four-speed manual transmissions, both Corvette options not made available officially until 1957. On top of that, Curtice's street-going SR-2 is powered by a 283ci V-8, which also first appeared for 1957, replacing the

All three Corvette SR-2s appeared together, for the first time since 1985, at the 13th annual "Corvettes at Carlisle" event in Carlisle, Pennsylvania, in August 1994. From left to right: Jerry Earl's car, now owned by Rich Mason of Carson City, Nevada; Harlow Curtice's "low-fin" SR-2, owned by Richard and Carolyn Fortier of Swartz Creek, Michigan; and Bill Mitchell's high-fin model, owned by Bill Tower of Plant City, Florida.

1956 Corvette's 265ci small-block. Both racing SR-2s now have bored and stroked small-blocks, Earl's car displacing 333 cubic inches, Mitchell's 336.

Were the three SR-2 Corvettes predicting the near future when built in 1956? Many have long believed the powertrain features were prototype installations. Apparently partly yes, partly no.

Still basically in original condition, Curtice's street SR-2 undoubtedly represents a yes. Since the last of the trio was built late in the 1956 model year, it's certainly easy enough to believe that the all-new production parts planned for 1957 were then available—however unofficially—to satisfy the whims of the division's top executive. Other than that, the only existing "hard and fast" documentation appears in a short September 1957 *Motor Trend* feature on Curtice's SR-2, which, considering deadline lead time, would have been prepared earlier that summer. *MT's* Walt Woron raved most about the car's four-speed trans—"whoever's responsible should take a deep bow," he wrote—representing the earliest known reference to that installation.

Hard and fast facts are not all that readily available concerning Earl's SR-2, although it is reasonably clear it was not originally equipped with fuel injection and a four-speed. Like most long-running race cars, various powertrain changes were made to the

first SR-2 over the years, muddying the waters even further. But according to noted Corvette collector Bill Tower, who now owns Mitchell's SR-2, Earl's car was basically stock (without a doubt it was carbureted) under that louvered hood when first built. Having contacted various insiders (including Bill Mitchell) to help him during the restoration of the second SR-2, Tower was told by a GM design staffer that, in the haste to simply complete the job, the original drivetrain—a dual-carb 265 V-8 backed by a three-speed—was initially retained. That combo undoubtedly didn't last long in the racer, but when it was replaced by more muscular equipment is anyone's guess.

As for Mitchell's SR-2, Tower was told it was indeed fitted, in prototype fashion, with a fuel-injected 283 V-8 and a four-speed when built later that summer in 1956. And reportedly, the 283 was then bored and stroked to 336 cubic inches by Smokey Yunick early in 1957 as part of various modifications made for yet another Corvette speed run down Daytona Beach.

The high-speed debut for SR-2 number one came in June 1956 at Elkhart Lake in Wisconsin, where first Jerry Earl and then Dick Thompson race tested the car. Both, however, discovered the same thing—the machine was just too heavy, what with all that extra "plushness" and such. Problems with the trunk-mounted, oversized, unbaffled fuel tank were also encountered. The only choice was to head back to the GM studio drawing board.

There, junior stylist Robert Cumberford—today automotive design editor for *Automobile* magazine—removed all the excess baggage: stock seats, heater, radio, windows and lift hardware, etc. Cumberford even donated a set of Porsche speedster bucket seats to help finish the job.

By that time, work was also finishing up on the second SR-2, the red racer Bill Mitchell had requested almost immediately after he had first set eyes on the Earl car. Built under Mitchell's direct supervision, this model differed here and there compared to its predecessor, the most prominent change coming in back. Instead of the small symmetrical decklid fin, the Mitchell car was fitted with a large tailfin structure offset to the driver's side. The so-called "high fin" functioned as both a driver's headrest and rollbar, and also housed the filler cap (hidden behind a flip panel) to a baffled 45-gallon fuel tank.

Compared to the basically decorative "low fin" on Earl's car, SR-2 number two's high fin obviously served more than one real purpose. Its functional aspects weren't lost on Jerry Earl, who had his racer's tail rebuilt along the lines (the two high fins are not identical) of the Mitchell machine's about the time the original SR-2 was brought back into GM Styling to be lightened. At a glance, the two cars then appeared much like twins. Closer examination, however, told the true tale.

Unlike its blue predecessor, Mitchell's red SR-2 was apparently fabricated "from scratch," not simply created by cannibalizing a standard production Corvette. It does wear an official 1956 VIN (vehicle identification number) plate with serial number E56S002532. But, again according to Bill Tower's Chevrolet design sources, that tag was apparently added later to help hide its "non-production" status from racing rulesmakers.

Evidence to this fact can be found with a ruler. Although it does use the same Sebring-inspired chassis features found on Earl's car, the highly modified frame under Mitchell's SR-2 has a three-inch wider track. A special cowl was required since the engine was mounted father back and offset to the passenger's side. Additionally, the fiberglass shell is considerably lighter throughout, meaning it was probably specially laid up by hand. Mitchell's design team also left off the twin simulated scoops found atop each fender of all 1956-57 Corvettes—including the two other SR-2s. This absence represents the easiest way to differentiate the second SR-2 from the first—after Earl's was converted from low fin to high, that is—in the various 30-something-year-old photos of the two siblings. This task was made more difficult during the time both were painted red—each has been resprayed more than once over the years.

Many other differences between the two racers came inside. Mitchell's men installed racing bucket seats right off the bat to help shave off pounds. The lightly skinned doors were also gutted, but were nicely trimmed instead of simply being left bare. Rudimentary pull-cords were used in place of the stock door handles.

Instrumentation again included a column-mounted tachometer, only this tach differed in design compared to its counterpart in the Earl car. Differing as well was the gauge layout in the stainless steel panel located in the center of the dashboard. Mitchell's car also received a special shifter plate identifying it as a "Chevrolet SR-2 Corvette." A wood-rimmed steering wheel and full carpeting completed the cockpit package.

The third SR-2 differed even more in comparison to its two track-ready forerunners. Watching as Jerry Earl's low-fin racer was going together in May 1956, Harlow Curtice decided he wanted a daily driver just like it. "How soon would you like that, Mr. President," probably came the reply from the Chevy design people who by then undoubtedly had the whole SR-2 trick down pat.

Curtice's SR-2 was completed in either June or July using a production-line Corvette, serial number E56S002636. Built only with street driving in mind, it was basically stock underneath, save for the aforementioned 1957 drivetrain installation. Outside, the third SR-2 received the typical extended snout and symmetrical low fin, only this ap-

Jerry Earl's SR-2 eventually became an SCCA racing champion, but not until Earl sold it to Nickey Chevrolet's Jim Jeffords late in 1957. Among track honors for Bill Mitchell's SR-2 was a 16-place finish at Sebring in March 1957. Here, the Mitchell SR-2 weaves its way around the airport course in Florida with two D-Type Jaguars off in the distance behind. *courtesy Bill Tower*

Interior treatments for the second SR-2, although stripped down, were still quite plush for a racer. Notice the non-essential trim pieces found at the shifter's base, on the dash and inside the door panels. Racing buckets, full instrumentation, a column-mounted tachometer, and a wood-rimmed steering wheel were included.

Although much mystery still exists concerning the three SR-2's powertrains, apparently the Mitchell SR-2 was equipped with a fuel-injected 283 V-8 backed by a four-speed, both prototype installations. Reportedly, Smokey Yunick bored this 283 out to 336 cubic inches early in 1957 in preparation for some high-speed runs down Daytona Beach.

The scoops at the back of the SR-2's cove panel on each door were functional on the two race cars (not so on the Curtice SR-2). They fed cooling air to the rear brakes through ductwork that ran through the door into this opening in the doorjam. From here, the air was directed into the vented backing plates at the rear wheels.

pendage was slightly larger and more rounded. A louvered hood and annodized aluminum side cove scoops were again used, only in this case they were non-functional. Unlike the non-functional hood added on production Corvettes in 1958, the simulated louvers on Curtice's car were recessed, a trick that required much reinforcement, which in turn added considerable weight. Reportedly, that hood weighed about 100 pounds.

Interior appointments included blue leather seats and door panels. Curtice's own "personal shade" of metallic blue paint was applied outside, complemented by whitewall tires on dazzling Dayton wire wheels. Topping it all off was a stainless steel removable hardtop.

A certified showboat that reportedly cost some $50,000 to build in the summer of 1956, Curtice's SR-2 did indeed make more than one appearance on a Motorama stage as a GM showcar before

the president began driving it on the street. About a year later, he sold it to a neighbor, who later passed it over to another buyer, and so on. Remaining in Michigan throughout its life, the third SR-2 managed to survive in decent original condition (discounting a 1960 minor accident repair repaint resulting in a slightly different shade of blue) over its life and has been in the hands of Swartz Creek's Richard Fortier for some 25 years now.

The two racing SR-2 Corvettes didn't have it quite so easy, the demands of racing being not nearly as forgiving as those of a quiet Sunday drive. Both were typically thrashed and went through various identities as their competition careers progressed.

Earl's SR-2 was the most successful of the two, although not while in the hands of Harley Earl's son. In November 1957, Jerry Earl and NASCAR founder Bill France took the first SR-2 to the Bahamas to race with longtime NASCAR ace

The trailing edge of the SR-2's door shows the opening (with seal) through which cooling air flowed from the bodyside scoops into the rear wheelhouse area.

This June 1956 photo shows the first SR-2's chassis, which probably came directly from one of the John Fitch's Sebring team cars. Notice the cerametallix brake linings and the special scoops mounted to each backing plate. While Jerry Earl's SR-2 was undoubtedly built with the twin-carb 265 shown here, it was soon retrofitted with a fuel-injected 331ci V-8, which it has today.

Curtis Turner doing the driving and Smokey Yunick typically behind the scenes with a wrench. After winning an early heat at the Nassau event, the Turner-piloted SR-2 lost its lunch on the main course, running off the road unable to return.

Earl then sold his racer to Jim Jeffords, who drove for Nickey Chevrolet in Chicago. Wearing Nickey's distinctive—if not slightly disturbing—"Purple People Eater" paint scheme, Jefford's SR-2 managed to roar off with an SCCA B/Production national title in 1958. Bud Gates Chevrolet in Indianapolis then raced the car in 1959 and 1960. From there, a couple more owners followed before the once-proud machine somehow ended up in a junkyard in Terre Haute, Indiana, in the early 1960s. It was later restored and today is owned by Corvette collector Rich Mason of Carson City, Nevada.

Bill Mitchell's SR-2 first showed up before the public eye when it arrived in Daytona on February 7, 1957, to once more kick up some sand like the first SR Corvettes had done the year before. As mentioned, Smokey Yunick was again present to help make the Mitchell car everything it could be mechanically. To help cheat the wind, the car was also adorned with a plexiglass canopy for the driver, a hard tonneau cover for the passenger side of the cockpit, full wheel discs and rear fender skirts. Up front, the headlights and large turn signal lamps were covered with conical farings.

With stock car veteran Buck Baker doing the driving, the odd-looking Corvette took top standing-mile honors in its modified class, turning an average speed of 93.047mph. Its flying mile speed was 152.866mph, second to a Jaguar D-Type.

Jerry Earl's SR-2 in its early "low-fin" days. Its racing debut came at Elkhart Lake, Wisconsin, in June 1956. Not long afterward, the car was returned to Chevrolet Engineering where it was lightened and modified with a "high fin" similar to the one used on Bill Mitchell's SR-2.

When first built, the Earl SR-2 featured an interior that re-sembled a showcar more than a race car. All this extra plush-ness meant a lot of extra weight. Accordingly, the car did not do well when first raced in this trim.

The Earl SR-2 after its conversion to "high fin" in the summer of 1956. Notice the stock Corvette scoops atop each fender; these features represent the easiest way to tell the first and sec-ond SR-2s apart—Bill Mitchell's car didn't have these.

Following in the early SR's tire treads, Mitchell's SR-2 then went south to Sebring in March as part of Chevrolet's competition Corvette team effort, highlighted by the Corvette SS's debut (see chapter five), however ill-fated. At the end of the 12-hour endurance run, one regu-lar-production-based Corvette ended up first in its GT class and 12th overall. Another production car finished 15th overall. While the Mitchell SR-2, piloted by Pete Lovely and Paul O'Shea, was right behind in 16th, a victim of too many pit stops. All told, the befinned racer did 166 laps totalling 863.2 miles at an average speed of 71.93mph. A decent effort, but as Bill Tower points out today, once a new, rebodied Corvette came along for 1958, the SR-2—with its obsolete image—became old news basically overnight.

Mitchell's SR-2 went into storage in a GM basement sometime in 1958. Chevrolet racer Don Yenko bought the car and campaigned it in the early 1960s, then sold it in November 1965 to Charles Knuth, who began restoring the well-worn racer. Tower took over ownership in 1979 and completed the job. Today, Chevy's second SR-2 re-sides proudly in Florida as part of Tower's impres-sive Corvette collection, which includes one of the five 1963 Grand Sports, Betty Skelton's 1956 beach racer and a 1967 L88.

Looking much like they did nearly 40 years ago, all three SR-2 Corvettes converged on the fairgrounds in Carlisle, Pennsylvania, in August 1994 for the 13th annual "Corvettes at Carlisle"

Too many pit stops plagued the Mitchell SR-2 during its run at Sebring in 1957. Here it speeds through a turn hot on the heels of a Maserati, the marque that won the 12 Hours that year.

event. It was the first time since 1985 that the trio was reunited; one can only wonder when they will come together again. One thing is for sure: those who were lucky enough to be on hand for the historic reunion this time were the privileged ones.

Chapter 5

Stillborn At Sebring
Duntov's Corvette SS

That this ill-fated racer today resides among the many four-wheeled legends at the Indianapolis Motor Speedway Hall of Fame Museum is only right, regardless of its meager track record. Twenty-three problem-plagued tours around Sebring's rough-and-tumble endurance course in Florida in March 1957. A few serious hot laps at General Motors' Arizona proving grounds in December 1958. A sizzling 155-mph sprint through the high banks to help celebrate the opening of NASCAR founder Bill France's Daytona International Speedway in February 1959. Not much more, certainly nothing less; that basically portrays the high-speed history of the Corvette SS in a steel-blue nutshell.

Yet there is much more to the SS tale, perhaps one of the greatest "what-if" stories in American sports-racing history. What if Chevrolet's movers and shakers had approached the SS project, designated XP-64, with all the fervor and financial backing then commonly displayed by their sports-car-building rivals in Europe? What if Zora Duntov and his engineering team had been allowed more time to design, test and sort things out? What if GM hadn't put the clamps on in-house competition development and support in the summer of

While John Fitch was leading a team of production-based Corvettes to Sebring in March 1956, Zora Duntov was busy with his own idea of how Chevrolet's two-seater should be raced. Later that year, he began planning for an all-out racing version of the Corvette to better compete with Europe's finest sports-racers. The result was the Corvette SS.

Chevrolet designated the SS Corvette project XP-64. The XP-64's cove panel shape represented the only real tie to the production Corvette from a tail view. Wheels are racing Halibrand knock-offs.

1957 following the AMA's ban on factory racing involvement? Then again, what if Duntov, Ed Cole, Harley Earl and the rest hadn't even tried?

Apart from everything the ill-fated SS didn't do, it did represent Chevrolet's first serious, all-out attempt to put the Corvette name on the international racing map, something that many at GM recognized could only help enhance the regular-production two-seater's image back on Mainstreet U.S.A. Although worn out today, a certain now-familiar gearhead adage definitely rang true in the Corvette's early days. Racing did, and still does, indeed improve the breed, if not through mechanical enhancements alone, then by direct association with a competition-winning, record-setting reputation. Although the SS never won a race—or finished one for that matter—it did serve notice in high-profile fashion that Corvettes and competition would always be companions.

Long recognized, but only then gaining real momentum in the 1950s as a major promotional tool was the relationship between racing victories at the track and popularity (translated: sales) on the street. Duntov himself had described this very relationship in September 1953 during an address before a meeting of the Society of Automotive Engineers in Lansing, Michigan. "All commercially successful sports cars were promoted by participation in racing with specialized or modified cars," he explained.

Continued Duntov, "even if the vast majority of sports car buyers do not intend to race them, and most likely will never drive flat out, the potential performance of the car, or the recognized and publicized performance of its sister—the racing sports car—is of primordial value to its owner. The owner of such a car can peacefully let everybody pass him, still feeling like the proud king of the road, his ego and pride of ownership being inflated by racing glory."

Improving both streetside performance and competition potential by adding V-8 power in 1955 had already helped boost Corvette popularity, saving the car from certain extinction. Further evolution clearly hinged on how well the Corvette would continue to compete, thus the reasoning behind the Daytona Beach speed runs and John Fitch's four-car assault on Sebring early in 1956.

But while Duntov had been there at Daytona to help establish the Corvette as a record-setting speedster, he kept his distance when it came time to go racing at Sebring with modified stockers up against Europe's best thoroughbred sports-racers, then led by Jaguar and Ferrari. He knew only a specialized racing machine bearing the Corvette nameplate would ever do if Chevrolet seriously wanted to compete on an international level. Nonetheless, it was a top class finish at the fifth running of Sebring's annual 12-hour endurance event that served as inspiration for Campbell-Ewald to proclaim in print in 1956 that America's only sports car truly was "the real McCoy."

Those popular ads aside, claiming title as this country's one true sports car was one thing. Qualifying the Corvette as a world-class sporting machine represented a whole 'nother hurdle entirely. Overemphasized (and soon to be overlooked) minor production class wins at Sebring didn't quite cut it. Nor would various Sports Car Club of America production-class victories to come, not as long as true international racing glory remained an unfulfilled goal.

Winning top honors at Sebring against the world's best specially prepared sports-racers, however improbable, of course would've been a step in the right direction in 1956. But in the opinion of Duntov and others, the only real glory awaited American challengers in France. The legendary Le Mans 24-hour torture test had long served as a launchpad to greatness for the sporting crowd, most recently for Jaguar's chaps who watched as their dominating D-Types took "Las Vingt-quatre Heures du Mans" laurels in both 1955 and 1956. And again for a third time the following year.

Introduced in 1954, the D-Type Jaguar relied on its purpose-built, slippery shell and state-of-the-art disc brakes (first used by Jaguar on its racing C-Types in 1953) to overcome its main rivals from Ferrari. A Briggs Cunningham-backed D-Type won at Sebring in 1955, and another finished third in the 12 Hours the next year. Interestingly, it was this particular Jaguar that helped directly inspire the creation of the Corvette SS.

Duntov wasn't the only one at GM to recognize the realities of international sports car competition. At Sebring in March 1956 it had become clear from chief engineer Ed Cole on down that Chevro-

let would never match up against the likes of Porsche, Ferrari, Jaguar, Mercedes, Maserati and so on with merely a modified production Corvette. Yet for an American manufacturer to become involved in an expensive, time-consuming, all-out race car development project was almost unthinkable. No U.S. automaker had tried such a thing since Studebaker had sent a five-car racing team to Indianapolis in 1932. And as spring was blossoming in Detroit in 1956 it appeared that streak would remain alive.

Leave it to GM Styling mogul Harley Earl. Again. Whether he meant it seriously or not, it was Earl who brought a yellow D-Type Jaguar—the aforementioned third-place finisher at Sebring—into his Styling studio in the early summer of 1956 with hopes of rebuilding it with a Chevy engine and racing it as an experimental Corvette. Some body modifications here and there, a switch to lefthand drive, and no one would've been the wiser.

No one, that is, save for Zora Duntov. Once he got wind of Earl's plan he quickly determined that such a hybrid would never fly. Besides, it would still be a Jaguar in disguise. Inspired into action, Duntov then immediately began work on a proposal for a purpose-built race car that would wear the Corvette name with pride. Amazingly, the proposal was quickly approved.

In July 1956, Chevrolet styling studio head Clare MacKichan began work on a clay model depicting a state-of-the-art race car with a low, rounded, bulging body looking a bit like the Jaguar Harley Earl had apparently used to wake up his cohorts. Had Earl's plan to modify that D-Type into a Corvette racer been a mere ploy to bluff Cole, Duntov and the rest into taking the situation into their own hands? Only his hairdresser knew for sure.

Not long after he had risen to Chevrolet's general manager position, Ed Cole, along with other division executives, were given their first look at MacKichan's clay near the end of July. All were impressed with the sleek, aerodynamic-looking shell, which resembled its regular-production Corvette counterpart only through its toothy grille and bodyside cove areas. From there, the XP-64 effort quickly escalated.

Official paperwork detailing the project was sent down from the top in September. According to those orders, XP-64 was to "be a competition racing car with special frame, suspension, engine, drivetrain, and body." Right out of the blocks, however, production plans were assigned very tight, incredibly short deadlines. Initial specifications mentioned building four XP-64 race cars, one intended for show duty in New York in December 1957, the other three to be completed in time to test and compete at Sebring—the stepping stone to Le Mans—the following March.

Cobbling together a show car for static display in less than three months may have been a possibility. Carefully crafting three additional

No nonsense here, save for perhaps the wood-rimmed steering wheel. The SS interior was certainly competition-ready, although it gave all new meaning to the term "hot seat" on race day at Sebring in 1957.

world-class racing machines from scratch at the same time, to be ready for action in only three months more, was completely out of the question given the money and manpower available. Final approval for the XP-64 project realistically involved only one race car, dubbed the Corvette SS.

Duntov's hand-picked crew immediately began assembling the Corvette SS's chassis and driveline, working night and day in a partitioned corner in Chevrolet Engineering. By October, MacKichan's styling crew had finalized the body design, which was then hand formed in magnesium, not fiberglass, to help keep overall weight as low as possible. Distinct exterior features included flush-fit headlamps and driving lights, tilt-up nose and tail sections, side-exiting exhausts, cooling louvers on the hood and rocker panels, semi-enclosed rear wheelhouses, and a somewhat futuristic headrest "pod" that doubled as a rollbar.

Duntov's engineers didn't even use fiberglass for the SS, opting for lightweight magnesium instead. This decision ended up helping assist in the SS racer's downfall at Sebring in March 1957 as the magnesium shell didn't dissipate heat well at all—both man and machinery were basically baked.

Power for the SS came from an injected 283 with aluminum heads and long, tuned headers. Additional weight-saving features included a special magnesium oil pan with baffles and fins to help cool the oil supply.

The original body design also featured a large, recessed inlet in the center of the hood area meant to feed denser air directly into the engine below. But wind tunnel tests in December showed that the inlet negatively disrupted air flow over the nose. Unable to find time to correct the design, Duntov had no choice but to delete the opening. Wind tunnel testing did, however, prove that the SS body exhibited minor lift characteristics and was comparable to the D-Type Jaguar as far as overall aerodynamic drag was concerned. The sexy shell was as superbly functional as it was good looking.

Deadline pressures also influenced chassis construction. To save time by keeping things as simple as possible, a tubular space frame design was chosen over the more desirable, and more complex, monocoque body/frame layout used by Jaguar. And to help beat the clock even further, Duntov's crew simply brought in a Mercedes-Benz 300SL tube frame to serve as a model. In the end, the cage-like SS chassis showed only a few minor similarities to the 300SL layout. One-inch-diameter chrome-moly steel tubing was used throughout, with the majority being round. Square tubing was used where some components were mounted to the frame. Weight for the tubular frame was a mere 180 pounds, a typical figure for race cars of the day. At 92 inches the SS chassis' wheelbase was a half foot less than the production Corvette. 102"

Suspension was by variable-rate coilover shocks in back, typical coils (with shocks inside them) at the nose. Up front, the hand-fabricated sheet steel A-arms, ball joints and forged-steel steering knuckles

looked very much like a regular-production arrangement. Two short links connected each end of an anti-sway bar to the underside of the lower A-arms. And steering equipment consisted of a specially built Saginaw recirculating-ball unit and a three-piece track rod. Steering ratio was a race-car-quick 12.0:1.

A tried-and-true de Dion axle was used in back instead of a fully independent arrangement, again to help save extra developmental time the engineering team simply didn't have to spare. Located by four lightweight (together they only weighed roughly six pounds) tubular trailing links, the curved de Dion steel tube axle wound its way from wheel hub carrier to wheel hub carrier behind a frame-mounted Halibrand quick-change rearend. Each trailing link used rubber bushings where they pivoted at their frame mounting points, while ball joints connected them to the de Dion axle.

The Halibrand unit was picked to once more help save production time, although Duntov's engineers only kept the existing housing, filling it instead with their own ring and pinion gears and quick-change cogs, all being specially machined and shot peened to resist fatigue. Interestingly, the differential inside that Halibrand housing was not a limited-slip unit. A limited-slip differential was prepared for the SS, but the appropriately beefed-up half shafts needed to couple it to the wheel hubs were not ready in time. The various quick-change gears available made for final drive ratios ranging from 2.63:1 to 4.80:1.

As for brakes, up-to-date discs would've certainly been nice, but such pieces were still in the developmental stage as far as GM was concerned. In their place, Duntov's men used the brawniest drum brakes they could fashion, combining Chevrolet's existing sintered cerametallix linings with big 2.5-inch wide shoes in equally big 12-inch drums—finned for cooling—at all four wheels. Ductwork at each wheel delivered the air for cooling those drums. And while the front drums were typically found nestled within XP-64's Halibrand aluminum knock-off wheels, the two rear units were mounted inboard on the Halibrand quick-change housing, a relatively simple trick that helped reduce unsprung weight in back.

Completing the Corvette SS's beefy brake system was an advanced vacuum-servo-controlled power booster setup designed to distribute stopping power proportionately from back to front to hopefully help avert rear wheel lock-up during hard stops. While front braking force was always relative to pedal pressure, a cockpit-mounted mercury switch controlled a valve that limited the power boost to the rear brakes. When the mercury in the switch responded to the negative g-forces created by deceleration, it electrically shut down that valve, meaning rear braking force would not increase beyond whatever level it was at that moment regardless of how hard the brake pedal was depressed. Front brakes would continue to work harder at

Both the nose and tail of the SS flipped up, in this case to allow access to the spare tire and rear coilover suspension.

stopping the car as the pedal went farther down, while the rears would not work too hard and lock the wheels once the tires began losing their grip as the tail started lifting. The idea sounded good. And it looked good on paper. Real world tests, however, proved otherwise.

Supplying the impetus to test those brakes was a race-prepped V-8 based on the Corvette's newly enlarged 283ci small-block. Inside, compression was kept at a definitely docile 9:1 to help ensure this powerplant would stick around for 12 hours at Sebring. Atop the iron block went specially prepared, lightweight aluminum heads featuring reworked ports and stock-size valves treated to some minor recontouring. Inserts were added to the exhaust valve seats to protect the relatively soft aluminum from the vicious pounding experienced at, say, 6500rpm. Intake valve seats, however, received no inserts.

Feeding this hungry V-8 was Chevrolet's new Rochester fuel injection setup, which itself sucked in the atmosphere through a duct running from the grille opening to the fuel/air metering unit. Reportedly, this ram-air setup translated into an extra 10 horsepower at 150mph. Also of great help were the tubular steel headers, hot hardware that not only shaved off unwanted pounds but also boosted output by another 20 horses. All told, XP-64's 283 produced 307hp at 6400rpm on the dynamometer. Redline was

The Corvette SS's tubular space frame was based, however minimally, on the design used beneath the Mercedes-Benz 300SL. Weight for this frame was only 180 pounds. Wheelbase was 92 inches, six less than the standard Corvette.

A Halibrand quick-change rearend, with Chevrolet-prepared internals, was chosen for the SS. And inboard mounted drum brakes were also typically added to reduce unsprung weight. The downside of this design was that the drums transferred unwanted heat to the differential housing and vice versa.

put at 6800 revs, 200 below the accepted safe limit for Chevy's little "hot one" in top performance trim.

Additional weight was trimmed by using an aluminum water pump and a special magnesium oil pan featuring a finned bottom panel and baffled internal passages to help keep the lubricant supply cool. On the scales, the entire SS power package weighed 450 pounds, about 80 less than a typical Corvette 283. Weight-saving aluminum was also used in manufacturing the bell housing, transmission case and radiator core. Overall, the completed SS weighed 1,850 pounds; Jaguar's D-Type carried roughly 100 more. A production Corvette was about a half-ton heavier.

A typical single-disc hydraulic clutch, beefed up with heavy-duty facings and stouter springs, delivered those 300+ horses to XP-64's aluminum-case four-speed transmission. Specially chosen for Sebring, first gear was 1.87:1, followed by 1.54:1 for second, 1.22:1 for third.

All in all, the finished product—painted a beautiful metallic blue—looked like a formidable warrior. Proving that fact was another matter. Needing basically every minute from the start of production in October 1956 almost up to race day at Sebring on March 23, 1957, to create his SS racer,

Duntov knew he'd never have the time to properly test the car and iron out all bugs prior to going into action. Luckily, he managed to squirrel away enough extra parts to assemble an unauthorized second SS, the so-called test "Mule." Almost enough. When the Mule arrived at Sebring for testing, it did so minus a few body panels and headlights. Its interior was incomplete and its crudely formed, white fiberglass shell helped bring total weight up 150 pounds compared to the magnesium-bodied SS. Available power was also down slightly.

All that aside, the SS Mule did its job well while running about 2000 test miles at Sebring. Various problems surfaced in time to make some changes on the blue SS. And as crude as the Mule looked, it proved itself to be quite formidable in action. During test sessions just prior to race day, legendary driver Juan Fangio took a seat behind the Mule's wheel and proceeded to rip off a lap time of three minutes, 27 seconds—about two seconds faster than the best lap run in 1956. Stirling Moss then took a turn and recorded a 3:28 lap. If the slapped-together Mule could run like that, what could its refined sibling achieve?

Then again, the blue SS was not as refined as it looked. Hampered from the start by the tight deadline, Duntov's men were still working on the SS

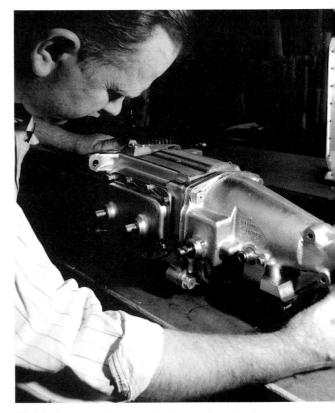

XP-64's four-speed transmission featured an aluminum case, a weight-saving idea that would become standard for four-speed production Corvettes in 1961.

Zora Duntov admires the SS racer's basic layout, with the many innovative features including finned brake drums, large ceramet-allix brake linings, and a baffled magnesium oil panel (at middle right on its side hanging over edge of table). In the foreground is the tubular de Dion axle.

even as it arrived in Florida via transport van at the proverbial last minute. Not only was the car not entirely ready to race, it was also without a driver. Fangio had been the original choice, with Moss considered as a co-driver. Moss, however, was already committed, while Fangio was released from a signed agreement with Chevrolet once it became clear the SS would never arrive at Sebring in time for proper testing and appraisal.

John Fitch was then asked to step in. Having led Chevrolet's production-based Corvette racing team to Sebring the previous year, he was again placed in charge of the stock-class competition effort in 1957. While his experience did indeed qualify him as a top candidate for the SS job, it was the time element that mattered most. Fitch wasn't just a good choice to pilot the SS at Sebring. On short notice, he was basically the only choice. And on even shorter notice, Chevrolet contacted 50-year-old Piero Taruffi—by Fitch's request—in Italy early in

the morning on Tuesday, March 19, asking him to co-drive the car. He agreed and was flown in just in time to take a few practice laps.

What Taruffi and Fitch discovered during the SS racer's all-too-short practice time was that the car was definitely a different animal compared to the Mule. First, the magnesium body helped keep interior heat levels almost unbearable, a problem that hadn't surfaced in the better ventilated (remember the missing panels) Mule. The Mule's fiberglass shell helped insulate the driver from heat, while the magnesium SS body served as a heat conductor. To compensate, various sections of the doors and rocker panels were cut away as part of an effort to let cooling air in and exhaust heat out. Extra cockpit insulation was also added, all to no avail.

Making matters worse were problems with the complicated brake system, which had worked fine for the Mule. Fitch and Duntov were still trying to repair those brakes 15 minutes before race time,

Racing rules required a top be at least available for a competition legal sports-racer in 1957, thus the reasoning behind this bubble, which was never used. That's Duntov doing the modeling.

again to no avail. Fitch even went so far as to warn fellow drivers of his stopping woes while lining up for the Le Mans-style running start that Saturday morning on the grid at Sebring.

Once underway, Fitch did manage to give it a valiant try, bad brakes and all. The SS ran with the best of them, turning one lap at 3:29, but soon fell behind as glitches took over. First came an unplanned pit stop to change front tires after only two laps—the right front had been badly flat-spotted when it locked up during Fitch's last-minute brake testing prior to the race's start. A few times around the 5.2-mile course and Fitch was back in with a dead engine, the result of a faulty coil connection that required some 15 minutes to identify and repair. The SS died again back out on the course, forcing Fitch to replace the coil entirely. Meanwhile, heat in the cockpit continued to be a major problem. Finally, a failed rubber bushing on one of the de Dion

Despite no authorization for a second SS, Duntov's crew did manage to cobble together a fiberglass-bodied test "Mule," which here undergoes testing in Michigan late in the winter of 1956-57. Although considerably crude compared to its magnesium-bodied cousin, the Mule wowed many during practice at Sebring with its speed potential. And it didn't fry its driver like the SS ended up doing to John Fitch.

The racing career of the SS lasted only 23 laps at Sebring in March 1957. Brakes problems, a coil failure, a broken rear suspension, and continual over-heating difficulties caused the car's demise. Here, U.S. Air Force "Flying Boxcars" stand by as the SS chases a D-Type Jaguar and one of the production-based 1957 Corvette racers.

axle's trailing links in back made the SS all but un-manageable. After only 23 laps—22 by Fitch, one by Taruffi—the SS was forced to retire from the race.

The Corvette SS clearly had shown some powerful potential, and even in failure did represent a remarkable achievement considering how little time was allowed for its creation. As John Fitch later wrote, "I felt that we had somehow been cheated, that if we had only been allowed another month, the wrinkles would have been ironed out." Others were also quick to note what the car could be given time to flush out the gremlins. "Without a doubt," wrote Autocar's Jesse Alexander, "Chevrolet [has] a car that could win Le Mans in the hands of the right driver... given a proper share of luck."

Ed Cole was also confident of the SS's potential despite the Sebring debacle in March, so much so he immediately approved a proposal for putting together a three-car SS team for Le Mans later that summer. Continued Alexander, "under proper guidance, a team of three or four of these machines with top drivers could put the United States on the sports-racing car map." But a Chevrolet-backed Corvette team did not make it to France in 1957.

Even as plans were being considered for an improved Corvette SS, word began to spread concerning impending action by the Automobile Manufacturers Association to squelch factory-supported racing activities. While the AMA "ban" on factory racing didn't arrive until June, GM officials had already announced in early May that they would be dropping any and all competition connections. Although clandestine underground support for certain racers did continue from both Chevrolet and Pontiac, high-profile projects like the Corvette SS were obviously doomed. The quick retirement at Sebring had been the end of the road.

The book on the Corvette SS, however, didn't exactly close there. Both the blue SS and the white Mule survived the GM axe, with the Mule's chassis resurfacing in 1959 as the base for Bill Mitchell's Stingray racer, a machine driven to competition glory by Dr. Dick Thompson. As for the unfortunate SS, it made it back to the track, too. In December 1958, Duntov's blue baby ran an incredible 183mph during testing at GM's proving grounds in Phoenix. Then in February 1959, Zora himself drove the SS around the new Daytona International Speedway's 2.5-mile high-bank, hitting 155mph along the way.

Eventually, the Corvette SS was donated to the Indy 500 museum, where it was refurbished in 1987. And when the National Corvette Museum opened its doors in Bowling Green, Kentucky, on Labor Day weekend in 1994, there stood the still-proud SS to help greet visitors in the main lobby, up front where it belonged.

Chapter 6

1958-60
Onward And Upward

While the AMA factory racing ban of June 1957 did cut short the SS racer's career and put the clamps on Zora Duntov's plans to expand the Corvette image onto the international stage, it did little to inhibit the continuance of that image here at home. Fuel injection, the Duntov cam, competition brakes—these and other hot performance parts remained on the Corvette options list in 1958 for anyone to add to their fiberglass two-seater. Whether or not these private owners then took their Corvettes racing was purely up to them. Many did, some with more than a little unauthorized "back-door" support from Chevrolet Engineering. Most prominent among these alleged "privateers" was Dr. Dick Thompson, who commonly led the way as Corvettes went on to dominate SCCA racing in this country during the late 1950s and early 1960s.

As for action off the track, Chevrolet's Corvette began, in 1958, a perceived progression even further away from the European sports car ideal as size and weight grew and styling started falling more in line with typically trendy Yankee tastes. Sports car purists may have cringed, but they couldn't deny the Corvette's increasing popularity among the American jet set. Sales continually jumped up after 1956; 3,467 that year, 6,339 in 1957, 9,168 in 1958, and 9,670 in 1959, the last year production failed to surpass the 10,000-unit prediction first made for 1954. That barrier was finally broken in 1960 when 10,261 Corvettes were built.

Corvette updates for 1958 included quad headlights, simulated louvers on the hood and equally non-functional "vents" at the leading edges of the cove panels. The paint appearing here, Charcoal, was a one-year offering for 1958 alone.

Distinguishing between those last three model years wasn't all that easy at a glance since the 29,099 Corvettes built between 1958 and 1960 were all based on the same restyled body that had replaced the clean, classic look of 1956-57. Simple, even elegant, the 1957 Corvette has long been considered by many bystanders, innocent or otherwise, as the best of the first-generation, "solid-axle" breed, thanks both to its ground-breaking fuel-injected performance and uncluttered, crisp lines. This car was, at the same time, wholly American and like nothing else then seen out of Detroit. All arguments temporarily shoved aside, it represented the epitome of the American sports car ideal. Or at least it did until the stunning Sting Ray came along for 1963.

Nonetheless, lasting impressions left behind by the 1957 Corvette shouldn't be allowed to overshadow what followed. Just because so many fiberglass fans loved, and still love the 1957 model in no way means the restyled 1958 went unloved. A few slings and arrows were thrown, yes, but overall responses commonly involved patting Duntov's engineering crew on the back as performance carried on every bit as strong.

Now with 290 horses, the top 283 fuelie V-8 (with improved fuel metering and warm-up mixture control) was again capable of powering the 1958 Corvette through the quarter-mile in a shade more than 14 seconds. From there down you still had the 250hp injected V-8, as well as the 245- and 270hp dual-quad 283s. Outputs for all four optional

A totally restyled interior was finally added in 1958. Dash modifications included putting the gauges and tach in front of the driver where they belonged, but they still remained tough to read.

As in 1957, the optional dual-carb 283 with the hydraulic cam (RPO 469) was rated at 245 horsepower. At 2,436 sold, RPO 469 was second only to the base single-car 283 in popularity in 1958.

Twin chrome bands running down the decklid serve as a quick reminder as to what year Corvette you're looking at—the were only applied in 1958.

Corvette engines would remain unchanged up through 1960, as would the base 283 four-barrel, which beginning in 1958 was uprated 10 additional horses to 230. New for 1958 was the position of the 283 V-8's generator, relocated from the driver's side to the passenger's in order to improve fan belt "geometry," in turn increasing that belt's "grip" around the water pump pulley.

Transmission choices carried over unchanged from 1957, and would remain so for 1959 and 1960. Standard fare was again the three-speed manual, with the four-speed and Powerglide automatic coming at additional cost.

Styling was where the 1958 Corvette tended to take it on the chin. Its very prominent chin. In keeping with a corporate-wide trend, Chevrolet's latest 'glass body sprouted an extra pair of headlights up front, helping inspire *Road & Track* to call the new model "too fussy." In *R&T's* opinion, "that supposedly hard-to-sell commodity, elegant simplicity, is gone."

Painted valve covers always signified the presence of a base Corvette V-8; optional engines received various style finned aluminum valve covers. From 1958 to 1961, that base engine was the 230hp 283 backed by a three-speed manual.

America's only sports car in all its glory in 1958—top performance that year again came from a fuel-injected 283. This Snowcrest White fuelie is one of 1,511 built in 1958; 504 250hp versions, and 1,007 more with the upgraded 290hp 283.

Along with those quad headlights, new frontal treatment included two large simulated air ducts (which became functional with the optional racing brakes) and enlarged bumpers that were now mounted directly to the frame instead of the body as in previous years. Long, chrome accents went atop each fender, where they would stay up through 1962. Rear bumpers were also restyled in a much more prominent fashion, and two unexplained chrome bands were stretched up and over the deck-lid. These bands helped set a 1958 Corvette apart from the similar 1959 and 1960 models to follow—that parallel chrome trim treatment got the boot after appearing for one year only.

Additional "fussiness" came behind the front wheels where simulated vents were added to the previously uncluttered cove panel's leading edges. This design would stick around, too, in this case up through 1961. One feature that didn't stick around was the readily identifiable new hood with its 18 fake louvers, an arrangement that at least reminded some witnesses of the SR-2's fully functional louvered lid. Like the trunk chrome, the 1958 Corvette's simulated louvered hood did not make a return appearance.

Overall, the restyled shell, at 177.2 inches, measured more than nine inches longer than its 1957 predecessor, most of that increase coming up front. Total width grew as well, from 70.5 inches to 72.8. Weight accordingly also went up, by 200 pounds to 3,080, making for the first time a Corvette tipped the scales at more than a ton and a half. It was this newfound heft, along with all those extra styling baubles, that had some Chevrolet insiders in 1958 joking about how much "Cadillac-like" the new Corvette had become.

The car was, of course, very much "unCadillac-like" from behind the wheel, where performance belied the 1958 Corvette's somewhat bulked-up image and an updated cockpit surrounded the driver with fresh flair. Gone was the same basic dashboard used since 1953 as designers finally responded to complaints concerning gauge location. All instruments were in 1958 moved to directly in front of the driver in a modern-looking, recessed pod arrangement. A larger speedometer, calibrated to 160mph instead of 140, was added, as was a new 6000-rpm standard tachometer (a 7000-rpm unit had been used in 1957) located in a relatively prominent pod directly atop the steering column.

Choosing either one of the two solid-lifter engines (270- and 290hp) meant that standard tach was exchanged for an 8000-rpm unit.

Additional updates included all-new inner door panels, a center "console" below the dash where the standard clock and optional heater and radio went, and a stylish "grab bar" across the concave area incorporated on the dashboard's passenger side. The steering wheel, however, was still basically the same sporty three-spoke unit introduced in 1956. And although upholstery was new, the seat design continued to leave many drivers sore and unsure of their placement in hard turns, problems inherent with the Corvette interior from the beginning.

Even Duntov admitted the new 1958 interior wasn't perfect by any means, the seats in particular. Instrument legibility was still on the tough side, but he preferred to point out that they did represent a marked improvement over what came before. That they did, although some weren't so easy to accept that rationalization. Nor was everyone particularly kind when it came time to acknowledge the deficiencies.

As in 1957, the lower performance fuelie V8 in 1958 featured a hydraulic cam and was rated at 250 horsepower. Minor modifications meant the top fuelie V-8, with its solid-lifter cam, was bumped up from 283 hp to 290. Price for the RPO 579 fuel injection setup was still $484.20.

Up front, the louvered hood used in 1958 disappeared once the 1959 Corvette debuted.

As veteran race driver Ken Miles wrote in *Sports Car Journal*, "in only two respects does the car fall short, and whilst the styling department is undoubtedly responsible for the miserably illegible instruments, I feel the engineering department is probably to blame for the totally inadequate seats. [These] are neither comfortable to ride in nor give any lateral support at all so that there is a constant temptation to drive round corners hanging on to the door with one hand in order to stay behind the wheel."

Miles did speak highly of the Corvette's maximum performance potential. As mentioned, all those hot pieces available in 1957 were still around in 1958. A Positraction differential with 3.70:1, 4.11:1 or 4.56:1 gears. Wide 15x5.5 wheels with their small hubcaps. And the race-ready RPO 684 package. Still priced at $780.10, RPO 684 again added quicker steering, stiffer suspension, finned brake drums with cooling scoops and cerametallix linings, and that somewhat complicated brake-cool-

Interior updates for 1959 included different style seat upholstery and the addition of a storage bin to the passenger's side of the dash.

ing ductwork that this time took in air through the two normally fake vents (functionally opened up, of course) added beneath the 1958 Corvette's quad headlights. How convenient.

As before, it was highly recommended not to rely on those heavy-duty brakes for everyday use, as Miles was quick to explain. "When cold, the cerametallic lining is ferociously unpredictable," he wrote. "For low speeds the slightest touch on the brake pedal almost pitches both drive and passenger through the windshield. At normal freeway speeds incautious application of the brakes results in a hasty and unexpected change of lane." That was the downside. "But at high speeds," continued Miles, "the brakes really come into their own and haul this great big automobile down from maximum speed with no sign of fade whatsoever, time and time again."

Few drivers, however, found the chance to discover firsthand the realities of Chevrolet's cerametallix brakes since only 144 Corvettes were equipped with RPO 684 in 1958.

The same could've been said in 1959 when another 142 buyers checked off RPO 684, this time priced at only $425.05. Cost was slashed by deleting all that extra ductwork used in 1957 and 1958, leaving the vented backing plates to do the brake cool-

ing on their own. On the other side of the coin, RPO 684 springs were stiffened further in 1959, which was probably only right considering the extra weight the Corvette had been saddled with the previous year. Spring rates went from 340lb/in to 550 in front, 125 to 145 in back.

New options for 1959 included stronger, high-speed 6.70x15 nylon blackwall tires—limited-production option (LPO) number 1408—and yet another brake package. This one simply featured special sintered metallic linings supplied by GM's Delco Moraine division. These metallic shoes didn't "eat up" the drums' inner surfaces as bad as their gnarly, ceramic-based counterparts did, nor did they work as poorly when cold. Metallic brakes were listed under RPO 686 at a cost of $26.90; 333 sets were sold in 1959, followed by another 920 in 1960.

Also introduced in 1959, on March 12, was LPO 1625, an oversized gas tank that upped the available fuel load from the stock 16.4 gallons to 24. This option's competition implications were obvious. Reportedly, Chevrolet had installed as many as seven enlarged 21-gallon fiberglass fuel tanks in 1957 Corvettes, but these cars were meant only for the track. LPO 1625 represented the first time John Q. Public could enhance his Corvette's range. Again, whether or not John Q. then used that increased range to run longer between pit stops on a race course of his choice was strictly his prerogative. Remember, Chevrolet wasn't involved in racing. No sir.

Logically filling up more space than usual behind the Corvette's bucket seats, the so-called "big tank" required the additional inclusion of RPO 419—the $236.75 removable hardtop—thanks to the fact there was not enough room left to mount the standard folding roof in its typical location. Yet another mandated modification involved the standard Corvette gas cap with its protruding tab or "handle," which wouldn't allow the filler door to close due to the 24-gallon tank's relocated filler neck. Assembly manual instructions offered a simple solution: "Rework cap by removing handle or bending it over to make it flat with surface of cap."

No production figures are available for the LPO 1625 option, but estimates claim less than 200 big tanks were installed between 1959 and 1962. Beginning in 1961, the cap clearance problem was dealt with differently as a lengthened neck was simply extended through a holed filler door, itself sealed to the body. A bright, smooth-faced cap with serrated grip edges topped off that neck, representing the easiest way to pick out a rare big-tank Corvette built in 1961 and 1962. But only if the original owner didn't cut down the neck and re-install the typical working filler door, something most apparently did due to the perceived unsightly appearance of the exposed cap. Very few exposed-cap big-tank Corvettes are known. In 1962, LPO 1625 was redesignated RPO 488, for which a production number is known—65.

Corvette production in 1960 surpassed the 10,000 level for the first time—that figure had been the original projection for 1954. Exact production was 10,261. By 1960, color combinations were almost endless, as the light blue convertible top on this Ermine White/Sateen Silver Corvette attests.

Among modifications made to the standard Corvette package for 1959 was the aforementioned deletion of the louvered hood and chrome decklid trim and the addition of 10 rectangular slots to the wheelcovers to help cool the brakes. Underneath in back, a pair of radius rods were added to tie each end of the rear axle more solidly to the frame. These trailing links helped at least partially cure the inherent shuddering and "wheel hop" problems common to solid-axle designs during hard acceleration. Early Corvettes were especially susceptible to these maladies.

Shock absorber mounting points were also moved to improve their damping effect. And the new 1959 shocks incorporated a nitrogen-filled bag inside to help prevent fluid foaming during hard use.

Inside, a convenient storage bin was added to the dash beneath the passenger-side grab bar,

and the door knob was moved farther forward with added convenience in mind. Seats were slightly reshaped to hopefully keep the driver's butt more firmly planted, incremental calibration of the instruments were better defined, gauges received concave lens to assist legibility, and the four-speed stick was equipped with an innovative, safety-conscious reverse-lockout mechanism. Shifts into reverse could only be made by squeezing a T-handle added to the four-speed lever. Twin sun visors were also introduced as an option, RPO 261, for the 1959 interior.

All these improvements and additions of course meant a corresponding cost increase. Priced at around $3500 with essentially no individual options offered (they were listed, but apparently were all included on every car built) to hike that price during its first three years, the Corvette was by 1959

Base price for a 1960 Corvette was $3,872, a relatively minor increase over the $3,500 asking price listed during the car's first few years on the road. Options, however, were plentiful, making the possibility of seeing a bottom line soar beyond $5,000 quite common.

being offered at $3,875 in base form. Options had begun growing in number after 1956. Two years later, putting a Corvette bottom line well beyond the $5000 level was no problem at all.

Few onlookers, apparently, were discouraged by this fact. "For all around performance per dollar, the Corvette is hard to beat," wrote Stephen F. Wilder in a *Sports Car Illustrated* review of Chevrolet's 1959 fiberglass sports car.

Motor Trend's Wayne Thoms came to a similar conclusion after comparing the 1959 Corvette with Porsche's latest open-air two-seater. "Which one is the best buy?" asked his article. "Depends on what you want in a sportscar," came his reply. "If getting a lot of performance from a precision-built, small-

Early Corvette seats represented another area of complaint for customers who wanted to drive a sports car like a sports car. Improvements were made, but the 1960 rendition still apparently left much to be desired. According to *Sports Car Illustrated* they looked "more buckety than they are, offering little side support."

Introduced in 1959, Roman Red was again the hot color of choice for Corvette buyers in 1960, with 1,529 cars of this shade sold, second only to Ermine White at 3,717. Priced at $16.15, the optional two-tone paint scheme was still around as well, listed under RPO 440. Production of Roman Red/white 1960 Corvettes was 779.

Production of the solid-lifter 270hp 283 Corvettes in 1960 was 2,364, making it the second most popular power choice behind the base 230hp V-8. Price for this twin-carb engine, RPO 469C, was $182.95.

displacement engine is intriguing, then the Porsche is the answer. If you like the idea of having one of the world's fastest accelerating sports cars, then pick the Corvette. Truth is, both are excellent buys. They're sturdy, reliable, comfortable and above all, fun to drive. What more can you ask of a sportscar?"

Apparently not much, considering Chevrolet simply rolled out an essentially identical model for 1960—and this after so many Corvette watchers had earlier concluded that much greater things were planned.

"The changes to the car in the last six model years are not so great as we think will come about in 1960," claimed a report in the January 1959 edition of *Road & Track*. "We predict that this will be the year of the big changes for the Corvette."

Prime inspiration for this prediction came from two main sources, the XP-700 Corvette built for GM Styling chief William Mitchell early in 1959 and the "Q-Corvette" project, kicked off in the fall of 1957. Basically a typical personally customized flight of fancy intended for executive use, the XP-700 showed off what many in the press though was the upcoming new Corvette look for 1960. As it was, Mitchell's dream machine did predict a styling change, that being the "boat-tail" design that debuted in 1961.

The highly advanced Q-Corvette, on the other hand, was apparently initially considered for production beginning in 1960. Early design

William L. Mitchell took over as chief of GM Styling in December 1958. Future feathers in his cap would include the 1963 Sting Ray and Buick's Riviera.

models featured a startling coupe shell and an innovative driveline incorporating an aluminum V-8 sending torque to a transaxle located at the rear wheels. By trading a transmission typically located behind the engine for a rear-mounted transaxle, Duntov's engineers gave the Q-Corvette a more balanced stance as weight distribution moved away from the normally nose-heavy production Corvette standard.

But in the end, the costly Q-Corvette project was shelved. Temporarily. While the transaxle idea never resurfaced as a Corvette feature, that low, sleek shell ended up leading to the creation of the stunning 1963 Sting Ray coupe. With nothing else left in the oven for 1960, Duntov was left no choice but to keep the existing Corvette cooking as best he could for however long it took to develop a real all-new model.

"1960 will go down as the Year of Speculation for Corvette, *SCI* not being the only magazine that was caught well off base on predictions of radically changed styling and construction," wrote Karl Ludvigsen of *Sports Car Illustrated*. "New-type Corvettes along the lines theorized had actually been proposed, but the terrific engineering concentration on the Corvair project literally left no time for other developments. From the exterior

One of Bill Mitchell's many Corvette playtoys was this styling fling, XP-700, which appeared in the spring of 1959. While it was a bit futuristic up front, it did foretell the design change to come for 1961 in back.

Now You See It, Now You Don't
GM Designer Francis Scott's Retractable Hardtop Corvette

In the beginning Chevrolet's Corvette was a true roadster. No exterior door handles. No side windows. A nearly fully functional folding soft top that was best left stowed behind the seat. When it came time to drive your 1953, 1954 or 1955 Corvette top-up in bad weather, everything was just peachy as long as you didn't mind a little typical dampness and a lot of wind noise.

British sports car buffs never seemed particularly bothered by such annoyances—but then they didn't mind being left in the dark by their Lucas electrics, either. American sportsters, on the other hand, have always differed considerably from their European counterparts. Call us spoiled, think us blouse-wearing poodle-walkers, we Yankees have long tended to expect as many comforts of home as possible in our automobiles, sporting or not. No compromises. No trade-offs. Clumsy, less-than-transparent side curtains and leaking, booming canvas tops may have once represented an acceptable price the sporting crowd paid for their driving excitement, at least in foreign car terms. But it became clear not long after the Corvette was born that if an American sports car was going to thrive in sufficient numbers on these shores it would have to better appeal to American sensibilities.

So it was the Corvette was equipped with door handles and crank-up windows in 1956. New as well on the options list that year was an attractive, definitely functional—if not somewhat difficult to mount gracefully—removable hardtop. So what if a co-pilot was required to make the transition from open-air

tourer to weather-proof status-mobile? There was no better way to have the best of both worlds in a sports car, right?

Wrong. Or at least according to GM designer Francis "Scotty" Scott. Inspired by a desire to both have his cake in hand and mouth, Scott contacted the U.S. patent office in September 1962 armed with his idea for a retractable hardtop design based on the Corvette. His design featured a full roof that simply retracted back and down into an oversized Corvette trunk, to be hidden away beneath a modified, forward-opening decklid. One minute a full-fledged hardtop. An honest-to-goodness convertible a flick of a switch later. Who'd a-thunk it?

The guys at Peugot for one. In 1936, they introduced what was probably the world's first regular-production, "split-personality," retractable hardtop model. Four years later, Chrysler's stunning LeBaron-built Thunderbolt show car also appeared with a retractable "hideaway" hardtop. Other Detroit show cars later featured similar retractable designs, and Scott himself contributed to one such GM Motorama machine very early in his career, which began in 1951. In his words, that Motorama project "was like fertilizer, it promoted the idea in my mind."

Additional promotion came in 1957 when Ford introduced this country's most successful attempt to combine wind-in-the-hair excitement with fixed-roof comfort. Built up through 1959, Ford's Skyliner featured a complex retractable roof arrangement incorporating three drive motors, four lock motors, eight circuit breakers, 10 limit switches, 10 power re-

Created by GM designer Francis Scott, this 1958 Corvette features a retractable hardtop that can be raised or lowered—here it is stowed away beneath the rear deck.

A push of a button and little help with the hands later and Scott's Corvette is a full-fledged hardtop. Scott borrowed various parts for this design from Ford, which marketed retractable hardtop models from 1957 to 1959.

The fiberglass top simply rolls down channels into the trunk area where it is housed by a rear-hinged decklid restyled to add more space in back.

One of the keys to Scott's design was this hinged rear glass, which was first rotated before the top moved to add additional clearance for storage beneath the rear deck.

"Scotty" demonstrating its lift-up rear deck in front of Francis Scott's Michigan home in 1961. *Francis Scott photo*

lays and 610 feet of wire. Dearborn rolled out 48,394 of these mechanical marvels during the retractable Skyliner's relatively successful, certainly short, three-year production run.

Francis Scott, however, couldn't have cared less about a Ford product. Corvettes were naturally his favorites, although he couldn't quite afford one. A new one, that is. A few years after advancing up the ladder into GM Styling in 1953, he bought a rolled-over 1954 Corvette and rebuilt it as his daily driver.

Then in October 1958 he paid $900 for another trashed two-seater, "a jumbled up ball of wrecked Corvette hanging on a tow hook." What was left of that white 1958 model was delivered to his home in Warren, Michigan, where Scott's second restoration project began. Only this time the job would entail something completely different.

"I thought up the idea as I was putting the car back together," remembered Scott. "The back end was so badly damaged—there wasn't a back end there. And I saw that a retractable hardtop would fit down into the trunk and it all started going back together that way. I had to do some head-scratching in the beginning, but generally speaking it just fell together."

Scott used no drawings or models while building his retractable Corvette. Only three or four templates were needed. He also borrowed a lock motor, two flex cables and a pair of roof latches from a Ford parts shelf, all Skyliner components. One other electric motor was used to drive the decklid hydraulics, but that was basically it as far as heavy hardware was concerned. Far less complicated than Ford's better idea, Scott's retractable hardtop simple rolled on rails down into the trunk. Clever layout of the roller channels and use of a "fold-down" rear window made the design a veritable breeze. "Crude but effective" was Scott's description. "Why complicate the design?" he continued. "It was difficult enough to achieve as it was."

Unlatching the top from the windshield header and rotating the rear glass horizontally started the sim-

ple process. A switch on the console beside the driver's right knee opened the hydraulically controlled, rear-hinged decklid, which in turn moved the top up and backwards. From there, the top moved manually on rollers back and down into the trunk. As the decklid lowered, its knee-action hinges—pieces that also anchored the roller channels in back—dropped the top even deeper into the trunk, supplying ample clearance for the lid when closed. Did wrenches ever appear in the works? "I don't remember it ever not working," Scott said.

Kicked off in late 1958 in, of all places, the front room of his Warren home, Scott's retractable 1958 Corvette was completed by October 1961. Bodywork included fashioning a restyled top and a modified tail to house that top when retracted. Extra personal touches included adding two large bumper bullets and relocating the exhaust outlets from the bumper ends to the lower quarterpanels directly behind the rear wheels. A fresh 1958 Corvette nose was grafted on in place of the original shattered 'glass and a gleaming black finish completed the job. Scott estimated he invested 3,200 man hours and about $2,600 in the "strictly shoestring operation."

Budget constraints help explain why Scott's retractable Corvette ended up looking so different in

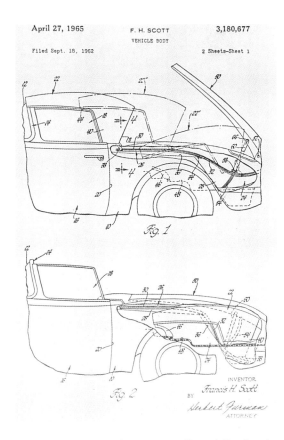

General Motors paid Scott one silver dollar for the rights to this patent. As for the idea of a retractable hardtop Corvette, little, if any thought was given to the idea.

Taken August 22, 1963, in front of GM Styling headquarters, this photo features more than 60 Corvette enthusiasts, all corporate employees. In front is Bill Mitchell with his Stingray racer; to his back is the XP-755 "Shark." Francis Scott is hidden in the left column with his retractable hardtop Corvette. His is the only quad-headlight car in that column, located sixth from the bottom. *Courtesy Francis Scott*

back. "Styling at the rear didn't quite satisfy me," he said, "but I didn't know what else to do to make it work. After I saw the car out on the street, it did look a little strange—I wished I had tried something else, but I'd already invested enough time in the project, I wasn't about to spend any more."

A little strange or not, Scott's creation did take a third-place trophy after its first big public appearance, a hot rod show in Detroit's Cobo Hall in December 1961. Soon afterward, Scott gave GM officials their own show in an executive garage. Present were Design Staff Engineering's Bob Lauer and Bill Mitchell himself. Recalled Scott, "Mitchell walked around the car once, completely ignoring me, said 'I'll be damned,' then just walked away. He was like that sometimes."

Lauer then suggested Scott contact the patent office. Patent number 3,180,677, detailing "a cover arrangement for convertible vehicle bodies," was issued to Francis H. Scott, assignor to General Motors, on April 27, 1965. GM traded Scott one silver dollar for the rights to the design, which were then filed away into obscurity.

As for the car, Scott drove it for about five years, then traded it for a used 1963 Chevy coupe. Details are sketchy until 1971, when Phil Wells, of Tallahassee, Florida, purchased the one-off retractable and began racing it. A pair of four-barrels had replaced the original-equipment single carb and white paint (with red coves) had superseded Scott's black exterior somewhere along the line. Wells sold the car to Miami's William Bruce in 1981. In March 1989, Terry Michaelis, of Pro Team Corvette Sales in Napoleon, Ohio, bought the unique Corvette from Bruce after seeing it featured in a national magazine.

Michaelis had seen the car once before in the early-1970s. "I knew [then this Corvette] was much more than someone's customizing project," he claimed, "as the cloth/resin layup was consistent with other GM concepts we've all seen before and since." Once in Michaelis' hands, the one-of-a-kind two-seater was quickly restored to "original" condition thanks to all-out efforts by Pro Team co-owner Fred Michaelis, body shop manager Dan Young, trim man Bob Hugo and ace assembly mechanic Billy Rodenhauser. "Scotty"—named by Terry Michaelis in honor of its designer/builder—was completed just in time for a special press introduction at a luncheon held August 27, 1994, during Carlisle Productions' 13th annual Corvettes at Carlisle extravaganza in Pennsylvania.

Although Francis Scott couldn't be there for the unveiling, he did supply much help to the Pro Team crew during the car's restoration. Having moved from the Detroit area to Oregon one month after his retirement from GM in October 1983, the 67-year-old forward-thinker still dabbles in out-of-the-ordinary design work, including a racing bicycle built for the Walt Disney movie "Ask Max." Scotty the man was, of course, happy to see Scotty the car come back to life. But he basically looked at it as old news. "I can't quite understand all this interest in the vehicle," joked Scott. "It was so completely ignored back then."

The car, maybe. But not the idea, as evidenced by Mitsubishi's recent release of its 3000 GT Spyder, the automotive world's latest attempt to marry carefree topless touring with fully functional, weatherproof practicality.

Another of Mitchell's personal rides was his Stingray racer, built late in 1958 using the chassis from the Corvette SS Mule of 1957. Many of the Stingray's lines would later reappear on the regular-production Sting Ray of 1963.

The Sting Ray's SS ancestry can be seen beneath its flip-up nose; compare this view with a shot of the SS's injected 283 V-8 in chapter five. *Bob Tronolone photo*

With veteran Corvette racer Dick Thompson at the wheel, Mitchell's Stingray became an SCCA champion in 1960. Here, Thompson works his magic at Riverside during the Times Grand Prix in October 1960. *Bob Tronolone photo*

After it was retired from racing, the Stingray was refurbished and put on the auto show circuit. Its debut on the stage was at Chicago's McCormick Place on February 18, 1961.

Along with Dick Thompson, other great Corvette racing names of the solid-axle era included Dave MacDonald, Don Yenko and Bob Bondurant, shown here at Riverside during the Kiwanis Grand Prix in July 1959. *Bob Tronolone photo*

and in all important respects, then, the 1960 Corvette is identical to last year's."

That's not to say the 1960 Corvette was devoid of improvements. Especially innovative was a standard rear stabilizer bar. Working in concert with a thicker (.70-inch) front stabilizer, this suspension upgrade meant stiffer springs weren't needed. Thus, higher-rate coils and leaves were dropped from the competition brake/suspension package formerly listed under RPO 684 in 1959.

In 1960, the corresponding option was RPO 687, which similarly included stiffer shocks, a quick-steering adapter, and finned brake drums with vented backing plates and cooling scoops. But this year, the brutish cerametallix linings were exchanged for the more civilized sintered metallic shoes previously listed on their own as RPO 686 in 1959. Also new was a clever 24-blade cooling "fan" mounted inside each brake drum. Price for the RPO 687 package in 1960 was $333.60. Production was only 119.

Dave MacDonald wheels his Corvette around the Marchbanks Speedway at Hanford, California, in September 1960. MacDonald would later die in a fiery crash at Indianapolis. *Bob Tronolone photo*

Easily the most important improvement came by way of the Q-Corvette's powertrain experiments, as well as the engine advancements used on the Corvette SS in 1957. Initially both the fuel-injected 283s offered for 1960, RPOs 579 and 579D, featured weight-saving heads with revised combustion chambers and larger intake valves. Cast out of aluminum, they helped shave off 53 precious pounds from the fuelie V-8. And, along with an enlarged injection plenum and an increase from 10.5:1 to 11:1 compression, these lightweight heads boosted fuel injection output from 250 to 275hp for the hydraulic-cammed RPO 579 V-8, and from 290hp to 315 horses for the solid-lifter 579D.

All this advancement, however, came basically only on paper, where advertisements touted this "major breakthrough in design and metallurgy" while announcing the arrival of the new 315hp Corvette for 1960. Casting difficulties quickly surfaced, as did problems with damage caused should the aluminum-head engine overheat. The "major breakthrough" was cancelled after only a few sets of these aluminum fuelie heads had become reality. Most were rejected due to casting irregularities. Left

back at the drawing board, engineers then rolled out the 250- and 290-horse injected 283s for one more appearance. Production in 1960 was 759 for the latter, 100 for the former.

Despite the cylinder head setback, aluminum did find its way elsewhere on the 1960 Corvette. A new aluminum bell housing cut off 18 pounds, while a few pounds more disappeared from 270- and 290hp solid-lifter powertrains thanks to the addition of a Harrison radiator also made of aluminum. All other hydraulic-cam Corvette V-8s in 1960 used copper-core radiators. And all cars, regardless of which radiator was present, also received a spacer that moved the fan nearly two inches closer to that radiator for better cooling.

Additional changes for 1960 were quite minor. Inside, seat upholstery was changed from a horizontal pleat to a vertical (as it had been in 1958). The door panel design was revised ever so slightly. And the 7000-rpm tachometer appeared without a total rev counter, a feature previously found on all Corvettes since 1953.

But even though news concerning the 1960 Corvette was limited on Mainstreet U.S.A., there

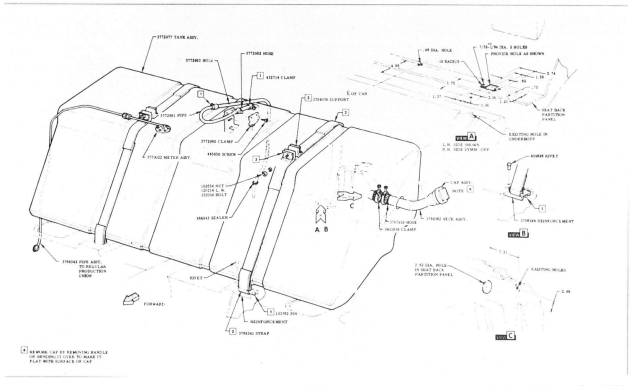

An oversized 24-gallon fuel tank became a Corvette option in 1959, listed under Limited Production Option (LPO) number 1625. In 1962, this option was redesignated RPO 488.

were big things happening overseas, where famed rich man racer Briggs Cunningham took a three-car Corvette team to France that year. A fourth competition Corvette also showed up for the prestigious 24-hour Le Mans event in June. Two of the three Cunningham cars failed to finish, although one of those did hit 151mph on the Mulsanne straight before melting its engine down after 207 laps. The third survived to finish eighth after turning 280 laps at an average speed of 97.92mph.

Without a doubt, eighth at Le Mans sure as hell beat tops in class at Sebring. And, in some respects, perhaps even an SCCA national championship. Even though it once more didn't represent a real victory, Cunningham's valiant effort at Le Mans in 1960 did impress more than one European as to the Corvette's status as a true sports car. Americans at the time were already sure.

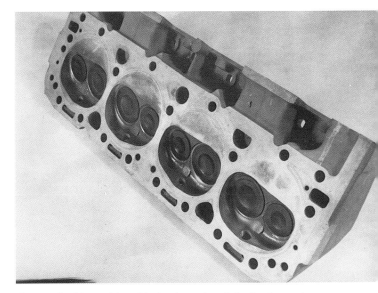

Duntov had hoped to add aluminum heads to the two solid-lifter 283 V-8s (dual-carb and fuel-injected) in 1960, but production difficulties shelved the effort. This same design was then re-issued in 1961, this time in cast-iron. *courtesy Noland Adams*

Chapter 7

1961-62
Last Of The Solid Axles

The Corvette's true "father," Harley Earl, retired in December 1958 after directing General Motors' styling affairs for three decades. During that time, GM had become a leader in looks among this country's automakers. Whether it involved innovations, trends, or fads, Earl's cars from Cadillac on down were always at the forefront as far as exterior design was concerned. As for Chevrolet's Corvette, it never once failed to turn heads during the 1950s.

Keeping Earl's legacy alive would be no easy task, something Harley himself recognized fully. By 1958, he had already groomed his successor, a Pennsylvania man Earl had discovered in 1935 doing automotive sketches while working for the Barron Collier advertising agency in New York. Six months after they met, William L. Mitchell had joined Harley Earl's Art and Colour studio. After another six months, he had soared to the chief designer's position at Cadillac. His first notable contribution to GM's rich styling tradition was the 1938 Cadillac Sixty Special, recognized as one of the best design efforts from the prewar years. By the time he had returned to the corporation after serving in the Navy during World War II, Bill Mitchell had essentially become Earl's righthand man.

New emblems and a modern grille sans teeth represented new Corvette styling features for 1961. Also new that year was the optional oversized fuel tank's (LPO 1625) exposed filler cap which protruded through the sealed filler door. When introduced in 1959, this option simply included a gas cap with its grip tab bent over or removed to allow clearance for the stock filler door.

"Boat-tail" styling at the rear of the 1961 Corvette represented the greatest exterior change since quad-headlights were added in 1958.

That Mitchell's future at GM later became entwined with the Corvette's was only natural considering his taste for racing. Already informed by Earl of his eventual ascension to GM Styling's top position, Mitchell in 1956 put a design crew to work building his own personal competition Corvette, the second of the three SR-2 models (see chapter four). Later, he managed to buy the chassis out from under the Corvette SS Mule (see chapter five), using it as a base for his second "private racer," the Stingray. Work on the Stingray began in Mitchell's secret "Studio X" in the winter of 1958. About the same time, on December 1, 46-year-old William L. Mitchell was officially named to replace the retiring Earl as the prime mover and shaker at GM Styling.

Even as powerful was he had become, Bill Mitchell still had to fight off considerable flak from above concerning the Stingray. Chevrolet wasn't involved in racing, he was sternly reminded by vari-

ous top level GM executives. But Mitchell was. So too was his Stingray, with more than a little support from Engineering insiders. GM Styling people, including a young designer named Larry Shinoda, had been of considerable help as well.

Debuting on the track at Maryland's Marlboro Raceway in April 1959, Mitchell's rebodied racer wore a bodyshell that borrowed most of its lines—courtesy of Shinoda's pen—from the sleek Q-Corvette project of 1957. Accordingly, the Stingray ended up predicting, quite accurately, the all-new Corvette look to come in 1963.

The musclebound machine also demonstrated a bit of what the ill-fated Corvette SS might've achieved had Zora Duntov and his men been given a second chance to iron out the bugs. With Dr. Dick Thompson at the wheel, Mitchell's Stingray roared to an SCCA national championship in the C/Modified class in 1960. Then, once retired from competi-

Adding LPO 1625 in 1961 also meant a customer had to order the optional removable hardtop, RPO 419, since the convertible soft top could not be installed in its typical location behind the seats.

In 1961, racing brakes came under RPO 687, which also added a quick-steering adapter. Included in the deal, priced at $333.60, were metallic linings, vented backing plates with air scoops, finned brake drums and internal cooling "fans." Heavy-duty shocks were also thrown in as part of the package. In this case, standard linings are in place on this 1961 Corvette to prevent unwanted wear to such highly valued equipment. The correct sintered metallic shoes are shown on the pavement.

Chevrolet had originally planned to up performance in 1960 by adding aluminum heads to the two solid-lifter 283 V-8s. Early advertisements even listed the two engines at 275hp (dual carbs) and 315 (fuel injection). But when the heads failed to make production, the standard power line-up for 1959 carried over. Not so in 1961. By recasting the same head design in iron, Duntov's engineers were able to make those power upgrades one year later. This is the 315hp solid-lifter 283 fuelie for 1961. Notice the missing ignition shielding—this particular fuelie came without a radio.

Convenience items like sun visors, windshield washers, a courtesy light and parking brake alarm were made standard equipment for the 1961 Corvette. Leg room was also increased that year thanks to a revised underbody panel that narrowed the transmission tunnel.

tion, the car was spruced up and in 1961 put on the auto show circuit, where it was a big winner as well.

Yet another eye-catching Corvette custom built for Bill Mitchell had appeared on the scene along with the Stingray in April 1959. Based on a stock 1958 Corvette, the XP-700 had been built that summer for Mitchell's personal use. It was a bit far-fetched up front with its extended snout and opened-up wheelhouses. In back, however, the XP-700 was quite pleasing, with inspiration for that look again coming from the Q-Corvette. Lines were more crisp, less rounded than the regular-production shape used in essentially identical fashion from 1956 to 1960. And four recessed taillights were mounted horizontally across the lower panel of the sharply creased tail. All in all it was certainly a fresh, modern-looking design.

And it was also the look Mitchell's stylists used to update the regular-production Corvette for 1961.

The new-for-1961 Corvette appeared quite similar up front in comparison to its quad-headlight forerunners of 1958-60. Changes included trading the chrome headlight bezels used previously for body-colored versions. And that bright, bullish grille with its nine "teeth" was finally retired after three years of service, replaced by a cleaner annodized rectangular mesh layout. "Corvette" block letters were also added across the nose above the grille.

From the rear, the 1961 Corvette was all new thanks to the addition of the XP-700's "boat-tail" design, which slightly expanded trunk space without increasing total length. And that boat-tail body not only totally transformed rearward impressions, but also changed the way the car expelled its bad

This somewhat soft shade, Jewel Blue, was another one-hit wonder as far as Corvette colors were concerned—it was only offered in 1961.

The old, reliable 230hp 283 was the standard 1961 Corvette powerplant, again backed by a three-speed manual transmission. Notice the barrel-shaped surge tank for the aluminum radiator—a new feature for all Corvettes in 1961.

air. For the first time, the Corvette's twin exhaust tips were not incorporated within its rear bodywork. Instead of exiting through the bumpers, as they had since 1956, the 1961 tailpipes turned down and dumped out directly behind each rear wheel, where, according to *Sports Car Illustrated*, "they rumble with a truly musical motorboat tone and beat a tattoo on the sides of the car you (frequently) pass."

Also included along with all that restyled fiberglass in back was a revised underbody panel featuring a narrowed (by about 20 percent) transmission tunnel. This, of course, meant an increase in interior room. Cockpit changes beyond that were minor—typically updated seat upholstery and door panel trim. Chevrolet did see fit to make the courtesy light, parking brake alarm, windshield washer and sun visors standard equipment for 1961. The first three of these features had been extra cost options since 1956, the last since 1959.

More optional power was a new 1961 feature as well. While the base V-8 was still the 230hp 283, and the 245- and 270hp dual-carb engines remained available at extra cost, the two fuel-injected powerplants were now rated at 275 and 315 horses. If these numbers sound familiar, they should, having been mentioned early in 1960 when Zora Duntov tried to

add aluminum heads to the Corvette's fuelie V-8s. For 1961, these big-valve heads were simply recast in iron and mated to the injected 283s along with the other modifications previously planned—11:1 compression and an enlarged injection plenum.

Along with this power boost came new RPO codes. Since its introduction in 1957, the fuel injection equipment had been listed under RPO 579 with various alphabetic suffixes determining the various performance levels and transmission applications. In 1961, the 275hp hydraulic-cam 283 fuelie became RPO 353, while the solid-lifter 315hp variety was assigned RPO 354. Price for either fuelie V-8 remained at $484.20. Production in 1961 was 118 for the 275hp engine, 1,462 for the 315hp 283.

As for the carbureted 283s, the 245hp (hydraulic cam) version retained the RPO 469 code used previously. The mechanical-cammed 270hp 283, however, was redesignated RPO 468. Prices for these two optional powerplants also carried over, $182.95 for RPO 468, $150.65 for RPO 469. Chevrolet in 1961 sold 1,175 of the latter, 2,827 of the former.

Another new feature for 1961 was RPO 242, a mandatory item for all Corvettes delivered in California. The large black hose in the center is part of a positive crankcase ventilation system, which superseded the existing practice of simply venting crankcase vapors into the atmosphere via a road-draft tube or such.

Another new grille, this one blacked out, helped set apart a 1962 Corvette from a 1961. Rocker panel moulding were also new for 1962, as was the cove panel "vent" treatment.

The Corvette base price went over four grand for the first time in 1962, reaching $4,038. Production jumped considerably, from 10,939 in 1961 to 14,531 the following year.

More fuel-injected horsepower wasn't the only thing new beneath the hood of the 1961 Corvette. Less weight also made big news as an aluminum radiator became standard and the RPO 685 four-speed's cast-iron case was traded for an aluminum one early in production. The lightweight transmission case saved 15 pounds.

First included along with the high-lift cam 283s in 1960, the aluminum radiator idea was revised for 1961 as a remote surge tank was used in place of an integral header tank. Looking much like a mini beer keg, this aluminum surge tank was mounted near the front of the driver's side valve cover. But not all 1961 Corvettes had this type radiator as Chevrolet first had to deal with leftover supplies of the previous year's header-tank units. This situation was explained in a factory bulletin:

"Approximately 1,700 early production 1961 Corvettes will be built with 1960 type radiators. One hundred ninety-two 1960 copper ra-

Chevrolet increased displacement for its V8 again in 1962, pumping the 283 up to 327ci. The base Corvette 327 that year was a 250hp version. Three optional 327s were offered two carbureted, one fuel injected.

diators will be used on Corvettes with standard equipment engines. One thousand five hundred 1960 type aluminum crossflow radiators, part number 3147516, will be used on all 1961 Corvettes after the copper radiator supply is exhausted. When the 1960 type aluminum radiator supply is exhausted, Corvette production will use aluminum radiator part number 3151116 on High Performance Engines and aluminum radiator part number 3150916 on all other type engines."

Completing the standard cooling system in 1961 was a temperature-modulated, clutch-controlled fan, a former Corvette option first offered in 1959.

Even with the various new standard features and its rear end makeover, the 1961 Corvette didn't go up in price all that much, its $3,934 base figure representing only a 1.6 percent increase over 1960's figure. Typically, all the same basic options available previously—bigger wheels, high-speed nylon tires, Positraction, metallic brakes, the RPO 687 big-brake/quick-steering package, oversized

fuel tank, etc.—again made it easily possible to drive a $5,000 Corvette off the lot in 1961. And this prospect once more apparently failed to discourage the Corvette faithful as another 10,939 of them doled out about four or five grand for a fiberglass two-seater that year.

What they got for the money represented the most complete, most refined, best balanced Corvette package to date. And the 1961 model wasn't bad looking to boot. Even *Road & Track's* Euro-conscious critics were finally impressed.

"Once upon a time, just a few years ago," began *R&T's* review, "owners of America's only sports car were on the receiving end of constant gibes from the 'sporty car set,' which held that the only thing the beast had to offer was drag strip performance. It would go like the wind (in a straight line, they said), but it wouldn't corner, it wouldn't stop, it had a boulevard ride, and a glass body. And it took 265ci (4.5 liters) to get that performance. Well, these derogatory remarks probably were true at one time. At least, some of them were. But Chevrolet

The same basic interior offered since 1958 made one last appearance in 1962 before the totally redesigned Sting Ray came along to wipe the slate clean. Once again, a different door panel design and an upholstery remake made up the noticeable changes inside a 1962 Corvette.

engineers have now achieved an excellent package, combining acceleration, stopping power, a good ride and handling characteristics whose adequacy is indicated by the car's race-winning ways."

Zora Duntov explained this achievement to the editors of *Sports Car Illustrated* in 1961. "Originally, our plan was to develop the car along separate touring and racing lines, as Jaguar did with the XK series on one hand and the C-Type and D-Type on the other," he said. "With this in mind we first introduced racing options, then the SR2, and finally the SS, which was intended to be our 'prototype' competition car. When this project was cut off, we realized we had to approach the Corvette in some other way. Since we could no longer build two kinds of Corvettes with different characteristics, we

Chevrolet offered its last dual-carb V-8 for the Corvette in 1961. In 1962, the two performance options this side of the top-dog fuelie featured large Carter four-barrels in place of the twin-Carter arrangement offered since 1956. This is the top carbureted 1962 327, rated at 340 horses.

Gettin' Their Kicks In A Corvette
CBS Television's Route 66

George Maharis (left) and Martin Milner of *Route 66* fame were together again during the "Route 66 Reunion" Corvette show, held November 6-8, 1987, at the Rocky Point Days Inn in Tampa, Florida. The Rocky Point Days Inn was once the Causeway Inn, which was where the final episode of the *Route 66* television show was filmed.

Nelson Riddle's jazzy hit theme was just fading out as Tod Stiles and a dozing Linc Case wheeled their way into Tampa's Causeway Inn in Stiles' 1964 Corvette. For Tod and Linc—alias Martin Milner and Glen Corbett—the Causeway Inn represented the end of the road. It was

unique CBS television program Route 66 played out its final episode in two parts, with the second half of "Where There's A Will, There's A Way" airing on the evening of March 13, 1964.

For four seasons, beginning in late 1960, Route 66 had carried American television audi-

The National Corvette Museum honors both the *Route 66* show and the famed highway of the same name. Statues of George Maharis and Martin Milner are part of the display.

ences on a journey over the length and breadth of this country. What made the show unique was that nearly all episodes were filmed on location. The adventures of Tod Stiles and Buz Murdock, later replaced by Linc Case, were not staged on back lots or in studios. Everyone—actors, the director, the crew, their families—all travelled from site to site, setting up to film in the towns the scripts were written for.

"We trucked everything from place to place," remembered production manager Sam Manners, "and when Route 66 visited a city it was a big event—like the circus coming to town. In four years on the road we never paid for a hotel and rarely paid for meals." During those four years, the Route 66 troupe filmed 116 episodes, sometimes working 16 hours a day, six days a week, travelling from Savannah, Georgia, to Cascade, Oregon; from Grand Isle, Louisiana, to Cleveland, Ohio; from Butte, Montana, to Tampa, Florida. All but one episode appeared on CBS network television. Number 101, "I'm Here To

Kill A King," about a political assassin, ironically was scheduled to appear the night of November 22, 1963. Network officials respectfully cancelled that episode following John F. Kennedy's assassination in Dallas earlier that day.

Producer Herb Leonard and writer Stirling Silliphant, who were responsible for Naked City, created Route 66 in the spring of 1959. The two came up with an idea to pair a poor kid from the streets with a wealthy preppie and then worked that storyline into a Naked City plot. Playing the part of the street kid was a young actor Leonard remembered from an earlier Naked City episode —George Maharis.

Once the "mini-plot" was aired, work began immediately on "Black November," Route 66's pilot episode. Although the show's "on-location" status, an industry first, was important to Silliphant, "Black November," meant to happen in the fictitious town of Garth, Alabama, was actually filmed in Concord, Kentucky, because a suitable site in Alabama could not be found. This was one

Buz Murdock (Maharis), at left, and Tod Stiles (Milner) atop Tod's Corvette on the way to Garth, Alabama, during the *Route 66* pilot episode, which aired on October 7, 1960.

of the few instances Route 66 was not shot at the advertised location, fictional or otherwise. Completed in February 1960, the Route 66 pilot was then purchased by CBS.

"Black November" established the premise for the Route 66 adventures, briefly explaining how George Maharis' character, Buz Murdock, "the poor street-wise kid from New York," teamed up with the son of his boss, Tod Stiles, who worked with Buz at the Stiles family shipping business during summer vacations away from prep school. Tod's dad then dies, the business fails and the two, both with no family left, then set out to see the U.S.A. in a Chevrolet, this one being the 1960 Corvette Tod inherited from his father.

Leonard originally envisioned the two travelling in a Ferrari, but decided a domestic car better fit the show's theme. Chevrolet was more than happy to supply a brand new example. Each year. While accepting how young Tod ended up with his father's Corvette following his death was easy enough, no explanation was ever given as to how he continued to find a new model every 12 months. Ah, the wonders of television.

As for the role of Tod Stiles, Leonard initially pared candidates down to two—Martin Milner and "a good-looking kid with some stage experience." While Milner already had television experience, his rival had very little. "We liked him," Leonard later recalled, "but he had a tendency to scream every time he got emotional." Milner was then chosen over the "good-looking kid," Robert Redford to you.

Redford later made various guest appearances on the show, as did many other well-recognized stars: Gene Hackman, George Kennedy, Robert Duvall, Alan Alda, Rod Steiger, Suzanne Pleshette, Joey Heatherton, Martin Sheen, James Brown, Lon Chaney Jr., Soupy Sales, and Rin Tin Tin to name just a few. Many made encore appearances, some more than once.

Starring as well with Tod and Buz were those new Corvettes, beginning with a Horizon Blue 1960 model, followed by a Fawn Beige example in 1961. Each succeeding Corvette used on the show was brown. Maharis himself also drove a black Corvette away from work, courtesy of the show's main sponsor. He first opted for a fuel-injected model, but the sometimes harsh realities of life on backroad America quickly helped change his mind. Local small-town garages more often than not were unable to service the fuelie, convincing him to switch to a carbureted Corvette in 1961. A family man with his wife and

Stars and stars-to-be were plentiful during *Route 66*'s four-year run. Here, Julie Newmar appears with Maharis in episode number 48, "How Much a Pound Is Albatross?"

kids along during location shoots, Milner passed on Corvettes, each year opting instead for a new Chevy station wagon.

On television, however, Milner was right there behind a Corvette's wheel every week delivering into our living rooms pieces of backroad America that have since all but disappeared. In Maharis' words, back then "the country had flavor." "You could drive 60 or 70 miles and find small towns with individual characteristics. Today, everything looks the same." Route 66 made a sincere effort to capture that flavor and feed it to viewers, many of whom would never taste it for themselves. So what if reality was stretched a bit. As Milner put it, "I think we inspired a lot of people, but it was a fantasy. You couldn't just drive into a town and get a good job the way we did." Maybe so, but what was wrong with a little fantasy once a week?

Apparently American television watchers didn't mind. By its third season, Route 66 had become a true ratings winner. The show "could have run for years," according to Leonard. "The people at Chevrolet and I had been discussing taking Tod and Buz to Europe after the fourth season. Route 66 could have been the first American series shot abroad." Instead, I Spy captured that honor as Route 66 fell by the wayside.

Problems began when Maharis contracted hepatitis early during third season filming. Then word got out he was squabbling over his contract. Milner was forced to appear alone as a recovering Maharis and network officials battled. Meanwhile, Buz Murdock's absence was not explained over the air as hopes for Maharis' return continued. Silliphant never did write in an end to Buz, "because we all felt [Maharis] might come to his senses and return to the show." He never did.

In his place, Silliphant eventually introduced Linc Case, fresh from a military stint, as Tod's new companion. Initially, Leonard had just the man for the job—Burt Reynolds. "But he didn't want to be any actor's replacement," said Leonard, who then chose Glen Corbett.

"Glen was a great guy," remembered Sam Manners, "and he tried very hard, but he just didn't have it."

Linc Case, played by Glen Corbett, was introduced in episode number 84, which aired March 22, 1963. Corbett replaced Maharis after a contract squabble took Buz out of the picture.

"We knew when George left the show it was over," added Leonard, "but we had our audience and the sponsor renewed us for the next season. Eventually, though, the audience got bored. It's really sad, when you think about the show's potential."

"It would be very hard today to duplicate what we did on Route 66," said Silliphant. "We were able to show the American character. The fact we were all over the map, with all kinds of people in every kind of situation, gave us a special richness. That would be difficult to show today since the country has become so homogenized. Places all look alike now—it's all Holiday Inns and freeways. Tod and Buz might not find the road so exciting anymore."

They'd also have a tough time finding what's left of the real Route 66, still the epitome of American backroads.

This is the #7 1962 Corvette as it looked when raced with great success by the late George Robertson. Robertson's fuelie even held its own up against Chevrolet's all-new Sting Ray at Daytona in 1963.

decided to give the Corvette buyer as much of both worlds as we could—to use our racing experience to combine in one automobile the comfort of a tourer and the ability of a racer. A big order, yes, but an interesting and worthwhile one. The 1960 Corvette was the first to reflect this thinking; the 1961 car is very similar."

SCI's review then went to call the 1961 Corvette "one of the most remarkable marriages of touring comfort and violent performance we have ever enjoyed, especially at the price."

Top reported 315hp Corvette performance for 1961 was a mere 5.5 seconds for the typically timed 0-60 acceleration run. The quarter-mile

Corvettes were kings of SCCA racing in the late 1950s and early 1960s, and would remain so until the arrival of Carroll Shelby's little Ford-powered Cobras in 1962. Some of those old warriors are still around, too—although it looks not at all like it did 30-something years ago, this Honduras Maroon 1962 fuelie was a very competitive production-class racer when new.

went by in 14.2 seconds at 99mph, and terminal velocity was listed at right around 130mph. Clearly, when you spent your hard-earned cash on an injected Corvette in 1961, you got what you paid for.

A Corvette customer received even more in return in 1962, the year the car's base price, at $4,038, went beyond the four-grand level for the first time. At a glance, not much changed as the same body used in 1961 carried over with only a few alterations. Mitchell's styling crew simply re-did the simulated vents at the front of each bodyside cove area and deleted the optional two-tone paint schemes and bright trim that had previously set off those coves. Minor additions included revised emblems, aluminum rocker panel mouldings and a black-out treatment for the grille.

Interior appointments were also all but identical, with restyled door panels and slightly revised seat upholstery representing the most notable updates. Heaters became standard in 1962, but could be deleted by checking off RPO 610.

Yet another of Bill Mitchell's flights of fancy, the XP-700 "Shark," was built in 1961 based on then-developing styling exercises for the upcoming 1963 Sting Ray. The name later became Mako Shark, then Mako Shark I once the aptly named Mako Shark II appeared in 1965.

Really big changes did, however, come under the hood, where the five-year-old 283 V-8 was bored and stroked up to 327 cubic inches. Four different 327s were available, one fuel-injected version followed by three others fed by single Carter four-barrels. The costly, somewhat complex dual four-barrel option was dropped after 1961, and it would be another five years before the Corvette would again be fitted with a multi-carb setup, that being the triple Holley two-barrels found atop the 435hp 427 big-block V-8 in 1967.

With a more potent hydraulic cam, 10.5:1 compression and small-valve (1.72-inch intakes) cylinder heads, the base 327 V-8 was rated at 250 horsepower, 20 more than in previous quad-headlight Corvettes. Adding a larger Carter four-barrel

and big-valve (1.94-inch intakes) heads produced the 300hp 327, RPO 583, priced at $53.80. The two top performance 327s both relied on the solid-lifter Duntov cam, big-valve heads and 11.25:1 compression. The Carter-fed version, RPO 396, was rated at 340 horsepower, while its injected counterpart, RPO 582, produced a healthy 360 horses. RPO 396 was priced at $107.60. RPO 582 typically cost $484.20. Production was 1,918 for RPO 582, 4,412 for RPO 396, and 3,294 for RPO 583.

Additional underhood modifications in 1962 included stronger pistons for the solid-lifter engines and distributor-driven tachometers on all four 327s. Previously, only the fuel-injected V-8s used distributor-driven tachs, with the carbureted cars featuring generator-driven rev counters.

Also, the Powerglide automatic was fitted with an aluminum case as weight consciousness continued. Still listed under RPO 313, the Powerglide was a $199.10 (itself, the same figure listed since 1959) option for the two lower performance, hydraulic-cam 327s only. The Corvette's fuel-injected V-8s had been limited to manual transmission installations since 1959. In 1962, a three-speed manual was once more a standard feature.

But few customers settled for that standard box. From its introduction in 1957, the Borg-Warner-built four-speed had grown in popularity each year. After only 664 were sold that first year, four-speed production made up 41 percent of the total run in 1958. That figure rose to 43 percent in 1959, 52 in 1960, and 64 in 1961. By the time the tire smoke had cleared in 1962, sales of four-speed

Corvettes had soared to 11,318, representing 78 percent of total production.

For the first time, two different T-10 four-speed transmissions were available at extra cost that year, both listed under RPO 685. The existing close-ratio four-speed, with its 2.20:1 low gear, was intended for use behind the 340- and 360-horse solid-lifter 327s. A second four-speed, this one identical save for its 2.54:1 low, was offered for the two hydraulic-cam V-8s. This wide-ratio box also could've been accompanied by a new 3.08:1 "highway" axle, a no-cost option listed under RPO 203.

Additional new options in 1962 included off-road straight-through mufflers (RPO 441), positive crankcase ventilation (RPO 242, mandatory on 1962 Corvettes delivered in California), and narrow

Extra body reinforcement represented one of the refinements made beneath the restyled (at least in back) Corvette body for 1961. *Courtesy Noland Adams*

whitewall tires (RPO 1832), which replaced the antiquated "wide whites" used up through 1961. And all the great go-fast options previously offered were 1962 carryovers, meaning top performance potential remained every bit as "violent" as it had been the previous year. "As always," claimed a *Car and Driver* review, "the fuel-injected Corvette engine is a sweetheart to drive."

More fiberglass fans than ever before found out just how sweet it was in 1962. With a second shift added at Chevrolet's St. Louis plant, Corvette production jumped up by 33 percent that year, reaching a new record of 14,531.

Credit for much of this increase could've easily belonged to Semon "Bunkie" Knudsen, who had came over from Pontiac to become Chevrolet general manager in November 1961 after Ed Cole had moved up to GM's ivory tower. Knudsen was no stranger to performance and racing, having resurrected Pontiac's image almost overnight after becoming PMD's general manager in 1956. Despite the AMA racing ban of 1957, Bunkie kept Pontiac heavily involved in competition-conscious performance developments. That he would continue such supposedly taboo tactics at Chevrolet was a foregone conclusion. And it was Corvette buyers/racers who would quickly benefit from his arrival.

Corvettes—most of them again "private racers" in name alone—continued to thrash their SCCA rivals on the track in 1962, as they had done in 1961. Dr. Dick Thompson's Corvettes won production-class national championships both years,

Duntov's CERV I at Riverside in November 1960. Although it probably could've raced, if GM sticks-in-the-mud would've allowed it, the CERV I vehicle served as an experimental test bed for various features, most notably the basic independent suspension layout applied in less complicated form to the 1963 Sting Ray.

This aluminum radiator became standard equipment for all Corvettes in 1961 once the supply of existing copper-core radiators was exhausted early in the year. In 1960, an aluminum radiator had been optional along with the two high-performance 283s.

while Don Yenko copped another in 1962. What better way to send off the last of the first-generation solid-axle Corvettes, easily the most successful of the fiberglass breed when it came to backing up its sexy image on the street with victorious results at the track.

By the time Knudsen had arrived, an all-new Corvette was already waiting in the wings. It would debut in the fall of 1962 with fully independent rear suspension and a sensational coupe bodyshell wearing low, flowing lines and hideaway headlights. Simply put, the stunning 1963 Sting Ray totally rede-

The top performance option in 1962 was once more a fuel-injected V-8, this time found under RPO 582. Atop the new 327 V-8, the Rochester injection equipment boosted output to a record high of 360 horsepower. Only one fuelie V-8 was available in 1962. Notice the plain plenum chamber, which first appeared in 1961. Previous fuel injection plenums had ribbed tops. *courtesy Noland Adams*

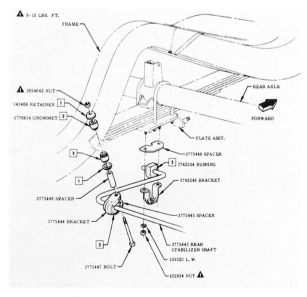

As in 1960, all Corvettes built for 1961 and 1962 came standard with a rear anti-roll bar.

fined the American sports car ideal, leaving the first-generation Corvettes to take their places as museum pieces. Then again, that Chevrolet had to produce such a superb automobile as the Sting Ray in order to supersede its existing sports car image surely represented an honorable testament to just how exceptional the solid-axle Corvettes were in their day.

Progress was the only challenger to ever leave these cars behind. Nothing on four wheels built in this country ever did. Nothing.

The solid-axle Corvette era came to an end in the fall of 1962 when Chevrolet introduced its sensational Sting Ray—for the first time a Corvette could be a coupe. Notice the attractive knock-off wheels. They were initially offered in 1963 then recalled due to production difficulties; they would finally debut in 1964.

Index